THE NATIONAL OBSTAC

NATIONAL PUBLIC STYLE

---

# OBSERVATIONS

ON THE

## PROBABLE DECLINE OR EXTINCTION

OF

## British Historical Painting,

FROM THE EFFECTS OF THE

## CHURCH EXCLUSION OF PAINTINGS.

---

RESPECTFULLY ADDRESSED TO

## HIS MAJESTY,

AND TO THE RIGHT HONOURABLE AND HONOURABLE THE
MEMBERS OF BOTH HOUSES OF PARLIAMENT:

## BY WILLIAM CAREY,

HONORARY CORRESPONDENT OF THE ROYAL INSTITUTE OF FRANCE;
HONORARY MEMBER OF THE ROYAL IRISH INSTITUTION
FOR THE PROMOTION OF THE FINE ARTS;
AND
HONORARY MEMBER OF THE ROYAL CORK SOCIETY OF ARTS.

---

*GRATUITOUS.*

---

London:
PRINTED BY HOWLETT & BRIMMER, FRITH STREET, SOHO.
1825.

TO

HIS GRACIOUS MAJESTY

# THE KING,

THE BENEFICENT PROTECTOR OF NATIVE GENIUS,

THE MUNIFICENT PATRON OF THE BRITISH SCHOOL

OF

**Painting, Sculpture, and Architecture;**

AND THE FATHER OF HIS PEOPLE;

AND

TO THE RIGHT HONOURABLE AND HONOURABLE

## THE MEMBERS

OF

## THE TWO HOUSES OF PARLIAMENT,

THE FOLLOWING

## OBSERVATIONS,

WITH A DEEP SENSE OF HUMBLE DEFERENCE,

ARE MOST RESPECTFULLY SUBMITTED,

BY

## THE AUTHOR.

*London, Feb. 25, 1825.*

" In a country where native energy is most abundant, we ask that professional taste and talent, and national patronage, be no longer confined to inferior objects ; but that our artists may be encouraged to direct their attention to higher and nobler attainments :—to paint the mind and passions of man, and to illustrate the great events which have been recorded in the History of the World."

*(Circular Letter of the Committee of the British Institution ; published by John Hatchard, Piccadilly, 1805.)*

" And it is, in this respect, worthy of observation, that *if we do not* ADVANCE, *we must* RECEDE; and that *when we cease to* IMPROVE, *we shall begin to* DEGE-NERATE."—*(Ibid.)*

" Your Committee cannot dismiss this interesting subject, without submitting to the attentive reflection of the House, how highly the cultivation of the Fine Arts has contributed to the reputation, character, and dignity of every government by whom they have been encouraged, and how intimately they are connected with the advancement of every thing valuable in science, literature, and philosophy."

*(Report of the Select Committee on the Elgin Marbles, 1816.)*

" Looking at the connection of the Arts with the glory of the nation, and with every thing that dignifies and ennobles man in his individual capacity, he deemed it consistent with the principles which a great nation ought to adopt, to stand forward as the Patron of the Arts, and to give largely to their support : *(cheers.)* —Ministers felt, that where A LARGE COLLECTION OF VALUABLE PICTURES WAS OFFERED FOR SALE, there were *many motives of liberal policy inviting the* FORMATION OF A NATIONAL GALLERY.

*(Speech of the Rt. Hon. Frederick Robinson in the House of Commons, Feb. 23, 1824.)*

" But, though unnoticed by the Public, *the Gallery of Mr. West remains* FOR YOU, *Gentlemen ;* it EXISTS *for* YOUR INSTRUCTION."

*(Sir Thomas Lawrence's Discourse to the Students of the Royal Academy on presenting the Prizes, 1823.)*

# OBSERVATIONS

## ON

## THE PROBABLE EXTINCTION

### OF

## BRITISH HISTORICAL PAINTING,

### &c.

---

.THE death of the late Mr. West occasioned an extraordinary sensation, and was followed, at his public funeral, by a signal testimonial of regret for his loss and of respect for his memory and genius. The celebrity of his works, the high rank, which that artist filled in the British School as the Founder and Father of Historical Painting; as the President of the Royal Academy of Painting, Sculpture, and Architecture; and as the first British Historical Painter, who had the honour to enjoy the personal favour of a British Sovereign, and the title of Historical Painter to the King, were circumstances, which, alone, justified the deep and general feeling. But there were other important circumstances attendant upon a life so full of years, and of professional honours, which increased the public concern.

B

The primary and distinguished share, which the late President had, in establishing the superiority of the British School in Historical Painting, the highest department of the Arts, over the contemporary Schools on the Continent, was one of those additional causes for national reflection. There was, also, much reason for melancholy apprehension, in the afflicting and well-known fact, that the chief part of the meritorious labours of his long life, forming a splendid collection of pictures from the works of the poets, from his own original fancy, and from sacred and profane history, remained *unsold*, in the venerable Artist's possession, at the time of his decease. The certainty that this magnificent collection, subject to all the contingencies of public apathy and neglect, is the sole inheritance which he had to bequeath to his family, is sufficient to alarm and intimidate every student, who might otherwise have looked up to historical painting as an honourable field of exertion, fame, and reward. The whole of the preceding circumstances, but chiefly, the last, and the uncertainty that awaits the magnificent collection of his *unsold works*, constitute the links, which, *in a national view*, inseparably connect the fate of WEST'S GALLERY and the celebrity of that great British Master, with the highest interests of the British School, and the glory of the British Empire. A mighty and long existing cause, alone, could have produced an effect so distressing and discouraging to British Students, and so likely to be converted into a lasting imputation upon the taste of the nation, by our foreign rivals and enemies. If it be a proveable fact of recorded notoriety, that the highest powers of the State formerly produced this cause of discouragement and national discredit, then it is fair to reason that every subordinate means and influence, although meritorious and praiseworthy, must prove ineffectual; and that no power, but the power of the King, the Government, and the Legislature, can remove the long existing obstacles to the successful cultivation of Historical Painting in the British Empire.

If a life so marked by enthusiastic application, so full of high performance, and so rich in celebrity as that of the late President, although constantly regulated by a wise and dignified economy in every branch of expenditure, has terminated in embarrassment, and has left to his sons no other property but the magnificent collection of his unsold pictures, subject to a continuation of disappointed hopes and accumulating uncertainties; a fact so humiliating to the British name and so appalling to British Artists, demands immediate and deep consideration. This is no season for general compliments. Mistaken compliments and flattering generalities have, already, produced much delusive and mischievous congratulation. The nation has been deceived, by the constant repetition of well-intended applause, into a belief that a liberal patronage of the *domestic style*, which includes our splendid triumphs in portraits, and in every branch of fancy painting, is a liberal patronage of the *public style*, which comprehends *historical painting only*. We have a right to be proud, and to exult in our rapid advancement in every department of the *domestic style*, because, in every variety of that style, the Public have afforded a competent encouragement for exertion: the leading professors did not stand in need of support from the Government, and have signalized their genius. But compliments on our advance in historical painting, are utterly destitute of foundation, if the speakers and writers mean to imply that there has grown up, within the last hundred years, such an improved state of patronage, as to afford a certainty, or even any reasonable hope, of reward, to the exertions of British genius in that high department of the Arts.

We must have done with that *erroneous classification*, which has, hitherto, confounded the DOMESTIC STYLE with the PUBLIC STYLE, and which has passed off, upon the unthinking, our triumphs in the former, as a triumph in the latter, at the very season when the want of patronage was withering and blighting the noble scions of genius in that field, and fast closing it against all future exertion. We must have done with self-congratulation and compliment; and must look the real state of things fairly and manfully in the face. Notwithstanding the munificent patronage of his late Majesty, and of our gracious Sovereign, in their personal character; notwithstanding the happy change in the public taste, produced by the noble show of British Genius, in nearly sixty annual exhibitions of the Royal Academy; notwithstanding the generous emulation excited in favour of British pictures in the *domestic style*, and the incalculable advantages to the British School, resulting from the taste, liberal prizes and persevering patriotism of that public-spirited body, the British Institution; notwithstanding all of these fortunate combinations, which we enumerate with sincere delight, we must admit the mortifying fact, that the insufficiency of private and national patronage for historical painting in this country, is so palpable as to render it unwise and unsafe for any young man of genius, or his parents and friends, to devote the prime of his years to study, in that high department of the Arts, with no other prospect but a life of public neglect and difficulties, and a failure of any certain provision for his family, at his decease.

This important subject has been generally touched upon in the best informed circles: but the constant succession

of commercial and political affairs, with the home occur-
rences of the day, which immediately affect the minds and
money-making interests of the million, have prevented it
from being sufficiently discussed. The surface has been
skimmed, but little more. We can only arrive at a fair
view of the consequences, to which the present want of
patronage for historical painting must inevitably lead, by a
brief but comprehensive view of the whole case. A calm
retrospect will enable us to decide, whether the state of
patronage for the *public style* has or has not increased in
this country, since the middle of the last century. It will be
seen that the most illustrious Personage of the State, alone,
had power to create the very limited historical patronage
which has existed during that long period. It will be also
seen that the royal example had little or no influence, even
in the court circle; and that nothing but historical painting
had power to excite the late King to take the Fine Arts
under his special patronage and gracious protection. If a
single historical painting, WEST's *Agrippina* landing with
the ashes of her husband, Germanicus, at Brundusium,
produced that powerful effect upon George the Third, in
1768; surely, in 1825, the fate of the splendid series of
West's *unsold* historical paintings, now on view in the noble
gallery erected by his sons, since his decease, must have a
lasting and decided influence upon every student in the
Royal Academy, and upon the most vital interests of that
high department of Painting.

In 1752, when Reynolds, after his return from Italy,
re-commenced his professional career in London, there
was no such art as British historical painting in England.
It was to be created. Here we have to repeat an
oft-repeated fact, that not only on the Continent, but
in England, a disgraceful prejudice prevailed against the

genius of Englishmen, amounting to a confirmed belief, that there was some disqualifying influence in the climate of this island, and in the minds and constitutions of Englishmen, which rendered them incapable of excelling in any works of invention, but those performances which are wrought by the mechanic arts. Notwithstanding the monstrous absurdity of this disgraceful opinion, it was received as an established truth. Among the celebrated foreign writers, who triumphantly promulgated this Anti-British notion, as a certainty, in their publications, it is quite sufficient to name the ABBE DU BOS, WINKLEMAN, MONTESQUIEU, and VOLTAIRE. But it is important to notice, that this gross prejudice did not originate with these eminent authorities. They only adopted and strengthened a general belief, which they found current on their entrance into public life, and which had existed during many generations. The splendour of their abilities and their popularity, successfully disseminated this Anti-British aspersion all over Europe, with a renewed force; and the envy of British superiority, in almost every other art of war and peace, obtained it ready credit: so that when *Reynolds* appeared, the arrogant and disgraceful assumption, that the people of England were inferior in genius to the people of the Continent, and were absolutely disqualified by nature from attaining to excellence in the Fine Arts, was received, as an axiom, by foreign Princes and People, by every foreign Court, foreign Academy, and foreign Literary Society.

Undoubtedly it was a truth that, at that period, England was far inferior to the nations on the Continent, in the Fine Arts; but it was a gross error to attribute that inferiority to any defect in the genius of Englishmen, which had originated in very different causes. The force of ancient political changes, and of conflicting religious opinions, beginning early in the reign of Henry VIII. and operating for two centuries, had not only rendered painting and sculpture extremely odious, and had excluded pictures and statues from Churches, but had engendered an almost incurable spirit of religious and political hostility to the Fine Arts in this country. So long as the Head of the Church and State, the Legislature, and the Clergy, esteemed the destruction of pictures and statues an act of loyalty and pious duty, which merited applause and pecuniary reward, it was not to be expected that Englishmen would devote their lives and genius to the cultivation of those obnoxious arts, as a means of professional fame, or even of professional livelihood. Who would take up the pencil and chisel, with the certainty of their inevitable consequences, neglect, contempt and poverty, instead of patronage, honour, and fortune! The whole spirit and authority of the Government, of the laws, of the Church, of public morals, and of public and private opinion, being directed against those productions of genius, as evil and disloyal instruments, they fell into entire disuse and abhorrence, in their very infancy in England, at the period, when, from opposite causes, from their being patronized by the temporal and spiritual Princes of Italy, and employed to embellish churches and public buildings, they were advancing to their highest glory in that country.

Thus the whole frame of government, the system of education, and the public institutions, which are the *only competent source* and *support* of the *public* or *historical style,* became, in this country, the active enemies and destroyers of painting and sculpture. This fact is not offered here as a novelty, but merely to impress the necessary truth, that, unless THE SAME HIGH POWERS, *which pro-*

*scribed* and *banished the Fine Arts, are as actively employed to re-instate them,* and *to open a constant field for* their *support,* it is in vain to expect that the public or historical style can continue, or ever flourish in England, although it may drag on something like a precarious and discreditable existence.

Here an important fact offers itself to our consideration. Although only devotional or sacred subjects in painting and sculpture, were proscribed by Edward VI. and Queen Elizabeth, yet when they were formally excluded from churches and public buildings, so dependent is the domestic style upon the public style, that the former sunk into insignificance, bordering upon utter extinction, soon after the latter was proscribed, and rooted out in this country. This consequence has not been sufficiently noticed. HOL-BEIN, NICHOLAS HILLIARD, and other painters, found employment in the reign of *Henry VIII.* and were patronized by that monarch: but under Edward VI. the English painters of portraits and familiar life, had already fallen into disrepute and poverty. Walpole has preserved an extract from one of Hilliard's letters, which shows the low state to which they were reduced. " Nevertheless, if a man be so induced by nature, and live in time of trouble, and *under* A GOVERNMENT *wherein arts be not esteemed,* and himself but of small means, *woe be unto him,* as unto an untimely birth; for, of mine own knowledge, it *hath made poor men poorer,* as amongst others many, the most rare English drawer of story works, John Bossam." This Hilliard painted Mary, Queen of Scots, and Queen Elizabeth, and the latter patronized Frederico Zucchero, and other portrait painters; but, even portrait painting fell into disuse, excepting at court. In every country where the *public style* is not *patronized,* although the *domestic style*

may be encouraged, and acquire, for a time, a flourishing
state, as, at present, in England, it is exposed to decline and
fall into an inferior taste from two causes: FIRST, from its
having no supplies of great principle, from daily and familiar
examples of *practice* in the public style: SECOND, from its
being supported by the patronage of the uncultivated million, and compelled to adapt its choice of subjects, and
mode of execution, to the liking and direction of persons
who are usually governed by the caprices of fashion, and
are, generally, more inclined to set a value upon enamel
surface, and that attention to minutiæ which wears the
appearance of high finishing, than upon the higher qualities
of breadth, pure taste, expression, character, and a fine
choice of nature.

The history of " that *most rare English drawer* of STORY
WORKS, in black and white, JOHN BOSSAM," may serve
for a specimen of the miserable poverty that attended
history painters, in the persecution of pictures, during the
reign of Edward VI. *Walpole* has published it, from
Hilliard's quaint manuscript, in which this artist is described as " one, for his skill, worthy to have been Serjeant Painter to any King or Emperor, whose works in that
kind are comparable with the best whatsoever in cloth, and
in distemper-colours; and belike *wanting to buy fairer*
*colours,* wrought therefore for the most part in *white* and
*black*; and *growing yet poorer,* by charge of children, &c.
*gave painting* CLEAN OVER: but being a very fair-condi-
tioned, zealous and godly person, *grew into a love of God's*
*divine service,* upon the liberty of the gospel, at the coming in of *Queen Elizabeth,* and became a reading minister;
only unfortunate, because he was *English* born, for even the
strangers would have set him up." Here the poor painter,
after having been driven by the church war against pic-

C

tures, to the cheap expedient of abstaining from colours, and painting in white and black, was at last forced to give "*painting clean over*," and to seek a pious asylum from beggary, in the church. It appears, that Queen Elizabeth not only had her portrait painted by *Lucas de Heere*, *Cornelius Ketel*, *Frederico Zucchero*, *Isaac Oliver* and *Mark Garrard*, but that she patronized *Lysard*, *who painted the history of Ahasuerus, for her*, (Walpole, vol. i. p. 217,) and Petruccio Ubaldini, an Illuminator on vellum, with many other English and foreign painters, whose names have been preserved by Vertue. These facts clearly show, that Edward VI. Queen Elizabeth, and their ministers, entertained a wish to preserve *domestic* and *ornamental painting* in this country. But the church exclusion of painting had excited such abhorrence and dislike, or indifference and contempt for pictures, that the public style and the domestic, perished nearly at the same time. The occasional arrival of foreign painters, to practise about the court, cannot be considered an exception to this statement.

In Greece, in ancient Rome, and modern Italy, painting and sculpture, *in their very outset*, were employed in the decoration of temples, and other public edifices. The subjects were suited to the buildings, of the highest class, religious, heroic, sublime and beautiful. The paintings, statues, and friezes being to be seen from below, generally at a considerable height, or from a distance, required broad effective masses, and grand ideal forms, to make a due impression upon the spectators. Every thing like a littleness of manner must have defeated the end of the artists. Hence, the public or historical style, upon a great scale, and on principles of grandeur, *preceded* and moulded the *domestic style*, and the latter, imbibing the great principles of the former, partook of its nobleness and elevation,

although its productions were upon a less expanded scale.
Thus, in Greece, and in ancient Rome, the ideal grandeur
of the public style was communicated to the small works
of art, in Painting, Marble, and Gems; which were the
productions of the domestic style. After the revival of the
arts in Italy, similar causes produced similar effects.
Painting and sculpture being employed, from their cradle,
to embellish the churches, municipal buildings, and palaces,
the *public* or *historical style*, as in Greece and ancient
Rome, preceded the *domestic style*, and the latter acquired
grandeur from the former. The highest class of subjects,
the highest powers of the mind, the noblest flights of the
imagination, and the most sublime objects, connected with
the love of country, and public and private virtue, were
embodied and called into action by the ancient artists, in
every progressive stage of the arts. But the course cannot be reversed; wherever the *domestic style* takes the
lead, the *public style*, unless sustained by very powerful and
constant patronage from the state, must be of a mixed,
inferior character, under the direction of individual patronage; subject to an indiscriminate choice of nature, and
deficient in ideal grandeur. This has been the case in all
those countries, where, in the sixteenth century, the religious changes were accompanied by an exclusion of painting and sculpture from the churches, and other public
edifices. Hence, in a part of *Germany*, in Holland,
Sweden, and Denmark, there being no *public style* to
purify and elevate the *domestic style*, the latter was formed
on the gross taste of the multitude, and never rose above
the imitation of ordinary nature. The works of the few
artists who painted history in those countries, are charac-
terized by a *Dutch taste*, a *Flemish taste*, or a *German*

*taste*, in contra-distinction from the nobleness and chastity of the Italian schools.

Here we must, again, repeat that the government of England having expelled painting and sculpture from the churches, about the middle of the sixteenth century, and the exclusion of painting having continued, with a few exceptions, to this present hour, it is plain that, without some powerful patronage and support from the government, the *public* or *historical style*, introduced by the patronage of the late king, must depend upon the caprices of fashion, or the fancy of the million, and fall into a feeble, bad taste, if not perish altogether, in the course of a few years.

Although the fierce spirit of hostility against the fine arts had lost its activity in the latter part of the seventeenth and beginning of the eighteenth century, the prejudices, in which that persecution had originated, maintained their ground; insomuch, that towards the end of George the Second's reign, a general apathy and disinclination to painting and sculpture formed a prominent feature in the British court, and in the character of the nobility and gentry, the learned professions, and of all those opulent classes of society which were in possession of wealth and power to patronize British genius. It was customary for the few British noblemen, who had acquired a taste in their travels on the Continent, to invite foreign painters and sculptors into England, whenever a commission was to be executed for the embellishment of their mansions. Owing to these long existing causes, it was an afflicting and disgraceful fact, that, at a period when the British statesmen and legislators, the British admirals and generals, the British fleets and armies, had extended the fame of British wisdom and valour through the globe—the country of Shakspeare and of Milton, of Locke, of Newton and Wren, could not produce any one historical painter to display the genius of Englishmen in that art. Thus, there being no English historical painters, and no English historical pictures, in 1752, when REYNOLDS finally established himself in London, after his return from Italy, the old inveterate prejudice, that Englishmen were disqualified by nature from attaining to excellence in the higher department of painting and sculpture, continued in full force, discouraging Englishmen of genius from the study of those arts, and reflecting unmerited disgrace upon the British nation.

Whoever entertains a hope of exciting the government to provide, in its wisdom and liberality, for the cultivation, or rather the preservation, of historical painting in this country, must not fail, distinctly and continually, without fear of being censured for *repetitions,* to hold up THE CAUSE, CHURCH EXCLUSION, which, from the reign of Edward VI. to that of George III. excluded England from historical painting; THE CAUSE, CHURCH EXCLUSION, which continues, and which (unless *immediately counteracted* by THE POWER OF THE STATE ITSELF) *will ever continue* to exclude her from any but desultory flashes of genius in that field.

From his conviction, that the highest department of painting was closed in this country, and rendered impracticable by CHURCH EXCLUSION, that illustrious artist, Reynolds, notwithstanding his splendid powers, his honourable ambition for the attainment of excellence, and his zealous endeavours for the advancement of the British school, did not deem it prudent to attempt history until *very late in life,* many years after he had been established in London, as the most eminent and popular portrait

painter of modern times, and some years after he had been
elected president of the Royal Academy. *Barry's* biographer bears evidence to this fact, that "*it was late in
life before Sir Joshua turned his hand to historical painting,*" (vol. ii. p. 260). BARRY, himself, on his arrival in
England in 1771, nineteen years after Reynolds had finally
settled in London, or twenty-five after he commenced his
profession there, found the President, in his forty-eighth
year, only resolving to enter the historical field,—"which
*shortly after took place.*" (Barry's Works, vol. ii.
p. 560.) This delay on his part fully proves his low
opinion of the public taste, or rather that the old dislike
and contempt for British historical painting pervaded
England. He commenced painting in London as early as
1746, and finally settled in the capital in 1752, after
having had the advantages of studying in Italy three years.
It is an undoubted fact that his first historical picture,
Count Ugolino and his Sons perishing of famine in a dun-
geon, was not finished and exhibited until the year 1773,
when he was in his fiftieth year, and twenty-seven years after
his first outset in the metropolis. During the last fifteen
or sixteen of those years, we have the testimony of Dr.
Johnson, of Reynolds's own declaration, and of his biographers, *Malone, Northcote,* and *Farrington,* that his income,
by portrait painting, amounted to 6 or £7000 a year, which
clearly shows that he was early in possession of a sufficient
independence to enable him to pursue historical painting,
if he had not considered that the exclusion of pictures from
churches, and the anti-historical state of the public mind in
painting, formed an insuperable bar to success. His
thorough knowledge of human nature, and his intimate
acquaintance with the prejudices of the time, taught him a
conviction, that if he had set out with painting historical

subjects, instead of thereby improving the public taste, he must have encountered poverty, and sunk himself in the opinion of those, who possessed the power of influencing society in his favour.

This fact is of importance. OPIE, in the Dictionary of Painters, mentions that Sir Joshua Reynolds was heard to say "he *adapted his style* to THE TASTE of the AGE," and "that a man does not always do what he would, but *what he can.*" This latter remark is to be found in his third Discourse: "Nor does a man always practise that which he esteems the best, but does that which he can best do." The two extracts have the same meaning. They leave no doubt that this great master *adapted his style to the taste of the age,* and yielded to the Evil Genius of historical painting, the church exclusion of pictures, without any vain attempt to struggle against it. In his fifteenth and last Discourse, after having eloquently expressed his esteem and veneration for the grand style of *Michael Angelo,* and having recommended the study of the works of that "divine man," he adds—"I have taken *another course,* one more suited to my abilities, and TO THE TASTE OF THE TIMES *in which I live.*" This is conclusive. He acted wisely for himself. If he had made an effort to fight against the *great national obstacle,* he must have sunk, like Barry, into neglect and poverty. The great national exclusion which forced Reynolds to conform his practice to the taste of the times, is at this moment in existence, and in full force against every young enthusiastic genius, who has the temerity to desert the taste of the age, and study the grand style in the historical department.

We have already remarked, that the domestic style, in Greece, ancient Rome, and modern Italy, emanated from the public style, and partook of its grandeur. But there is no instance of a taste for the public style having been diffused by the domestic style, in any nation in which paintings were excluded from the churches. If the portraits of any great ancient or modern master could have wrought the latter effect, those of Reynolds and Gainsborough would have produced it. But the contrary was notoriously the case. The domestic style, which, in its most popular branch, employs the pencil of Genius in preserving the resemblances of our relations and friends, deservedly exercises a general dominion over all orders in society; because it offers a virtuous gratification to the kindred affections, a pleasing homage to our self-love, and speaks a delightful language, that every where finds an interpreter in the human heart. The vulgar attempts to decry portrait painting are founded in selfishness and ignorance. In England, where the family ties are so strictly regulated by moral and religious feelings, portrait painting, at present, is more justly valued and encouraged than in any other part of Europe. But, although this charming department of the arts exercises so universal a sway within the social circle, it has much less influence over the highest powers of the mind, by which *public morals* are promoted, the love of country is fostered, and that exalted sense of *public duty* roused, which prompts to great and noble actions.

From reflections founded in the experience of ages, we again proceed to facts. George the Second, from 1746 to 1760, the year of his decease, had seen many of Reynolds's fine portraits, and had also heard of his fame; but they failed to excite that monarch to notice the painter, to employ his pencil, or to extend his patronage to the fine arts. The grand landscapes of WILSON, and the rural scenery and rustic figures and cattle of GAINSBO-

ROUGH, made as little impression at court, if ever heard of there, and were unnoticed by the public. HOGARTH, who, as a moral satirist in modern life, has never been approached, and whose Marriage-à-la-Mode and Lady's Last Stake evince the high and varied powers of his pencil, was despised and decried as a painter. He derived his fame and income from his engravings. George the Second was distinguished for his undaunted courage, sagacity, and affection for his subjects; but it is stated that he had no taste for poetry or painting; and the nation was as little affected by the finest performances of the four great painters just mentioned. REYNOLDS, excepting in his professed line of portrait painting, was not employed. His admirable fancy portraits and family groups failed to produce any taste for history painting in the nation. Not a solitary instance of a commission given to him to paint an historical picture occurred during his eight years' popular practice in London, during this reign. GAINS-BOROUGH's landscapes and rustic figures remained unsold on his hands, or, when exposed to the hammer, sold for less than the price of the canvas; he was obliged, with an indignant scorn of the public, to take refuge from debt and difficulty, in portrait painting, for a livelihood. WILSON, in mean lodgings and poverty, could not, with all his genius, make out a living, except by hawking his pictures among the low furniture-brokers, for whatever they were pleased to give for them. Strong as the domestic style was in this reign, in the varied powers of REYNOLDS, WILSON, GAINSBOROUGH, and HOGARTH, it made no impression on the people in favour of British history painting.

GEORGE THE THIRD, in the first eight years of his reign, from 1760 to 1768, had seen a splendid series of

D

admirable portraits, in single figures and family groups, exhibited by REYNOLDS and GAINSBOROUGH, in the annual exhibitions of the artists. There can be no doubt but that his majesty was struck by their unrivalled grace, beauty, elegance, and enchanting truth of nature. The king had also seen a number of admirable landscapes and rustic groups by Gainsborough, with a succession of Wilson's grandest productions. We want words and space to express our high sense of those three great masters' fine performances. The *domestic style* was then in its glory in this country; for Reynolds, Wilson and Gainsborough had advanced to their highest excellence in that style. But it is an incontrovertible truth, that they failed to call forth any public feeling for British history painting, or to awaken a desire in the royal breast to create a British school in that high department of the arts; to found a Royal Academy, or to set an example to the nobility and gentry, by extending his patronage to painting, sculpture, and architecture, as instruments of national improvement, elevation and glory.

Here we refer to facts proveable by incontrovertible public documents. The printed catalogues of the annual exhibitions, from 1760 to 1768, contain a list of the fine pictures exhibited by Reynolds, Gainsborough, and Wilson during those years. If any portraits, landscapes, or fancy groups of portraits, or of rustic figures from nature, could have overcome the inveterate prejudice against British history painting, excited by the long established CHURCH EXCLUSION OF PICTURES, and have roused England to a public feeling for that high department of the arts, as a means of moral instruction and national character, the works of those three great masters in the domestic style must have had that happy effect. But› although their unrivalled specimens of the *domestic style* immortalized the genius of those three great British painters, and nobly prepared the way for agreeable fancy subjects, it is a record of notoriety that they altogether failed to produce a public taste or feeling for history painting in the mind of the king and the nation. His majesty, although in 1768 he had been eight years on the throne, had never honoured Reynolds with an interview, nor employed his pencil. It has been truly stated (by OPIE,) that, during his practice in London, "at his table, for above thirty years, were occasionally assembled all the taste, talents, and genius of the three kingdoms; men who were remarkable for their attainments in literature or the arts, for their exertions in the pulpit or at the bar, in the senate or the field:"—MALONE, BURKE, NORTHCOTE, and FARRINGTON confirm this account. Yet, among the mass of illustrious statesmen and divines, legislators, admirals and generals, noblemen and gentlemen of the highest rank and fortune, talents and attainments, who were personally intimate with Reynolds, there was not one, from his first outset in London in 1746 to 1768, who had given him a commission to paint *an historical picture.*

Again we refer to the printed catalogues of the Annual Exhibitions, to show that Reynolds did not finish and exhibit his Count Ugolino until the year 1773: even then it was a mere chance which induced him to paint that first essay in history. NORTHCOTE, FARRINGTON, and CUMBERLAND, his friends, have established the fact, that the picture of UGOLINO did not originate in the mind of Reynolds; it was suggested to him either by BURKE or GOLDSMITH, and was painted without a commission. It is, also, known that the idea struck his literary friend, casually, when passing through his picture gallery, on seeing a head, painted from a well-known model, as a study of colouring and character, but intended for no more than a lesson of improvement. The chance remark of the moment, "*the expression of that head reminds me of the Ugolino of Dante*," was not designed as a hint for Reynolds to work the supposed miracle of converting a small piece of canvas into a larger, and to hammer out a single head into an historical picture. The hint, however, was not thrown away upon Reynolds, who had been then nearly five years President of the Royal Academy, and felt himself called upon, as head of that national institution, to exhibit some specimen in history. He had the small canvas inlaid upon a larger piece, to make room for the figures of the dying sons, and thus changed a study of a head, or rather a portrait from individual nature, into his first attempt at historical painting. It is certain, also, that after that fine picture had been exhibited, REYNOLDS received so little encouragement from all his great and noble friends, to exchange the popular and lucrative practice of portrait painting for history, that his *Ugolino*, although praised and admired, lay a long time unsold in his gallery upon his hands. While his admiring friends gave him credit for powers, (in the words of *Edmund Burke*), "*equal* to the *great masters* of the *renowned ages*," they were contented to let those high powers lie dormant in their noblest field, from 1746 until some years after, 1773, when his Ugolino was exhibited; they called for no higher demonstration of his admirable genius than their portraits, either in single heads, figures, or fanciful groups. Even to the last year of his life, this *anti-historical* spirit remained in full force with few exceptions.

Again we state facts. Of his very few historical pictures, or those which have been incorrectly classed as historical, the greater part were painted for foreigners, or for commercial men in this country: of the small remainder it is uncertain whether he ever received a commission for more than five or six from English noblemen or gentlemen. They were painted on the precarious chance of finding a purchaser among the visitors of his picture gallery. The Ugolino we have noticed as a spark of historical fire, struck out by chance. His Infant Hercules strangling the Serpents, was painted on a commission for the Empress of Russia, for £.1500, the highest sum ever paid to him for a picture; and thus the fame that could not abate the anti-historical prejudice begotten at home, by *church-exclusion*, reached the cold regions of the north, and was there honoured with peculiar distinction. Mr. Barry and Mr. Prince Hoare justly class this picture, which forms a principal ornament in the Imperial Palace at Petersburgh, as Sir Joshua Reynolds's chief historical work. *Prince Potemkin* gave him a commission for the Continence of Scipio, and also for the Snake in the Grass. *Count d'Ademar* purchased the Girl with a Mousetrap. *M. de Calonne* gave him a commission for Mrs. Siddons in the character of the Tragic Muse. *Noel Desenfans* purchased the Girl with a Cat; and the Girl with a Bird's Nest, and a Boy praying was purchased by *Monsieur Chaumier*. All the historical and fancy pictures here enumerated were painted for or purchased by *foreigners*, who paid homage to that power which his own countrymen overlooked. The Vestal Tuccia, the Holy Family, and the Gleaners, were painted on commissions for Mr. *Macklin*, as a commercial speculation; and he received similar commissions from *Alderman Boydell* for Robin Goodfellow, Cardinal Beaufort, and the Cauldron Scene in Macbeth. When we take away the preceding pictures and those fancy

subjects which he made presents of, or which remained unsold at his death, and when we consider the spirit of the
time, there is strong reason to believe the current opinion
that this great master did not receive ten commissions for
fancy or historical paintings, from every other rank and order of his countrymen, in the whole course of his forty-six
years' practice. We have not been able to obtain any certain proof of his having received five. For evidences of
this utter disinclination to give any employment to British
historical painting, we confidently refer to the lists of his
pictures, published by his several biographers, and to the
affirmation of his surviving contemporaries.

It is, also, a memorable fact, that, although all the most
eminent literary men, who flourished at the same period,
were in habits of friendship and intimacy with Reynolds,
they partook so largely of the anti-historical spirit of the
day, in painting, that their various publications bear no evidence of any effort or desire to abate that gross prejudice
or to excite a public feeling in favour of history painting.
The works of Edmund Burke, Dr. Johnson, Goldsmith,
Sheridan, Malone, Cumberland, Murphy, Garrick, and all
his other literary friends, are evidences that, on this particular point, they were frozen up by the *spirit of the age.*
They formed the power which influenced the periodical
press of the realm, but they never directed that formidable
engine against the CHURCH EXCLUSION of pictures.
They never employed their energies to introduce a public
taste for British history painting. The Throne and the
Senate, the Church and the Bar, the Literature and the
Press, the landed, the monied and the commercial interests,
were steeled by the same prejudice, during the first eight
years of the late reign. After this mass of testimony, it
may appear unnecessary to add this characteristic fact;

Malone mentions that Sir Joshua Reynolds had lived " on terms of great intimacy" with Edmund Burke, for more than thirty years. Yet, we find that BURKE, with all the theory of the sublime and beautiful in his head, was dead at heart to the interests of historical painting. Like the rest, he never gave any higher employment to the pencil of the great master, his friend, than that of painting his portrait, and even that but a little below the bust.

If Raphael, Michael Angelo, Correggio, and Titian, had been born in England, and had confined their pencils from the year 1760 to 1768, to painting portraits, fancy subjects, and landscapes, they must have failed to make an impression in favour of history painting. If Reynolds had devoted his pencil to history in 1752, when he finally settled in London, without the patronage of the crown, he must have lived in obscurity and indigence, and died in want. He must have sunk under the *anti-historical spirit of the age*, which, with respect to the fine arts, was formed by the *Church exclusion of pictures*, and which spirit overruled every other consideration of reason, public improvement, and national glory.

We have already observed, that GAINSBOROUGH was in the flower of his life, and professional excellence, from 1760 to 1768. He painted a series of his very finest pictures during that period. Many of them by their beauties, remind us of the style of Rubens, Murillio, Hobbima, Ruysdael, Everdingen, and Wynants. But they were then so undervalued, and so rarely purchased, even at prices which little more than paid for canvas and colours, that he, too, must have lingered through a life of neglect and indigence, if he had not made his timely escape from painting landscapes and rustic figures, and found full employment for his pencil in portrait painting.

Of WILSON's fate, let Fuseli, the eloquent Professor of Painting, speak for us: "He (Wilson) lived and died nearer *to indigence than* ease, and *as an asylum from the severest wants incident to age,* and *decay of powers,* was reduced to solicit the Librarian's place, in the academy of which he was one of the brightest ornaments." SHEE, with manly sympathy, adverts to this great master's sufferings:

"————————— While kind too late
Relenting Fortune weeps o'er Wilson's fate,
Remorseful owns her blindness, and to Fame
Consigns with sorrow his illustrious name."

"The place of librarian to the Royal Academy, the whole emoluments of which amounts but to fifty pounds per year, was conferred upon him to *eke out a mere subsistence !!!*"

It has been observed, that the pictures of REYNOLDS, GAINSBOROUGH, WILSON, and HOGARTH, now sell at as high prices as the works of "the great masters of the renowned ages." This rise in their value does honour to the purchasers, and is a proof that the public taste, in the *domestic style,* is much improved. But it is no proof at all, that a taste for the *public or historical* style, exists in this country. An argument from the high prices for the works of the illustrious dead, is too frequently offered under circumstances which prove an indifference to the meritorious works of the living. The very mention of such an evidence, suggests a recollection of the fact, that high prices were paid for the real or reputed works of the great old masters, in London, at the very time when a number of the finest productions by Gainsborough, Wilson, and Hogarth, were painted, without patronage, under every discouragement; and that, when painted, they lay unsold upon the artist's hands, who could not obtain a purchaser for them, at the lowest prices, or at any price.

But, if this *posthumous* rise in price for the fine works of *Reynolds, Gainsborough, Wilson,* and *Hogarth*, were the only proof that the taste of the British public has advanced within the last sixty years, it would prove very little. We rejoice that the taste of the public has improved in portrait, landscape, familiar life, and every other class of subject, in the *domestic style.* But we must own our fear, that there the account of improvement ends. To prevent too great a reliance upon those *posthumous* high prices, we refer to a fact. The works of *Raphael, Michael Angelo, Correggio, Titian,* and their great contemporaries, continued to rise in estimation and price in Italy, while the public taste, and the style of the Italian schools, rapidly declined. About the middle of the eighteenth century, when the public taste, and the style of the Italian schools, had sunk to their lowest declension, the fine painting and sculpture of the great masters, in Leo's golden days, were purchased at the highest prices, and held in the highest estimation, in that country.

Here we close our main proofs, that the DOMESTIC STYLE, including portraits, familiar life, fancy subjects, and landscapes, although sustained by the genius and vigorous practice of REYNOLDS, GAINSBOROUGH, WILSON, and HOGARTH, four of the greatest masters of the British school, wholly failed, from 1746 to 1768, during the last fourteen years of George II. and the first eight years of George III. to overcome or make any impression upon the obstacles to the public style of history painting, arising from the exclusion of painting and sculpture from the churches; and also failed to create a taste for historical painting in this country.

E

There was also at that period, a numerous body of British artists, in the various classes of the domestic style. One hundred and forty-one of those painters were members of "The Incorporated Society," in 1765.

Having arrived at this important point, two serious questions arise:—

FIRST.—Does not the great *national obstacle*, to the public style of historical painting, the exclusion of pictures from churches, exist in as full force in 1825, as it did in any of the years from 1746 to 1768 ?

To this, we may venture at once to reply—It does.

SECOND.—As REYNOLDS, GAINSBOROUGH, WILSON, and HOGARTH, with *one hundred and forty-one painters* in the domestic style, wholly failed, from 1746 to 1768, to make an impression upon that national obstacle to the public style; we ask, are there now in England, any four artists in the *domestic style*, SUPERIOR to those four great masters?

To this, also, we may frankly answer, that, as far as we have had opportunities of ascertaining the public opinion in amateur circles, there are not now any four living British artists in this country, superior to Reynolds, Wilson, Gainsborough, and Hogarth.

Therefore, it is plain, that the *domestic style* is, at present, as incapable of overcoming the national obstacle to the *public style* as it was from 1746 to 1768; and

We shall proceed to show that unless the Government, by some wise, speedy, and liberal measures of permanent patronage, will open a field for the encouragement and support of the public style, the historical style introduced by his late Majesty, in the person of WEST, in 1768, must decline and wholly perish in this country.

But, be it remembered, we are compelled to deny that,

the domestic style can create a taste for the public style
in any country, where paintings are excluded from the
churches and public buildings.  We again repeat our conviction, that the domestic style, however it may flourish for
a season, must gradually decline and fall into a bad taste,
unless invigorated and chastened, by a continual inter-
course with practical examples of the public style, executed by contemporary artists.  It is not enough to form a
NATIONAL GALLERY, enriched with fine examples of the
public style, by the old masters, for the inspection and
study of young artists.  The French, in the time of Louis
XV. when the meretricious affectation and empty facility
of BOUCHER, were extolled as models of grace and masterly execution, possessed the fine Italian specimens in the
Orleans Gallery, and in the Royal Collections in Paris and
its vicinity.  We have, also, already noticed, that with all
the great examples of the Vatican in view, the arts declined
in Rome, until the sickly mannerism of *Sebastian Concha*
and *Trevisiani*, the flashy bravura of *Antonio Pellegrini*,
and the dry servility of *Pompeo Battoni*, found disciples in
the schools where RAPHAEL and MICHAEL ANGELO
had taught; and patrons in the palaces, which their genius
had embellished.  These instances are quite enough to
show, that artists, like other men, do not form their style
upon what they see, or read, of past ages, but by the
manner or style which is in fashionable practice in their
own time.  We, again, anxiously repeat our well-matured
conviction, that unless the domestic style be derived from
the public style, and chastened by it, the former must be
moulded by the uncultivated taste of the million, and be
obedient to the heartless and frivolous caprices of fashion.
Wherever the public style and the domestic style are not
patronized, and do not flourish together, the latter must

decline. Artists in the same class and school, invariably
fall into an unconscious imitation of each other, until the
school dwindles, as the race of the noblest animals dege-
nerates, when the breed is too long confined to one stock.


# PART II.


THE preceding facts are essential materials in the British
annals of the eighteenth century. They are absolutely
necessary for the formation of any distinct view of the
present state of the British school. But many of them
have been hitherto kept out of view, by some writers,
through negligence, and want of research; or they have
been slightly noticed by others as isolated circumstances,
of little importance, from which no salutary inference has
been drawn. Like the stones for a building, hewed from
the quarries and laid in heaps, they have been accumulated,
by certain authors, with no other view but that of gratifying the rage for anecdotes, or swelling out their volumes.
Fortunately, the memoirs of Reynolds have been written
with commendable zeal and ability, by very eminent men,
to throw, what Sir Thomas Lawrence has so justly termed,
" a dazzling splendour " round the name of a painter
immortalized by his genius, by the profound philosophy of
his admirable Lectures, and by the dignified suavity of his
manners, which raised his profession in the public opinion,
and rendered him an object of general esteem and affection. The world is indebted to the biographers who
have so meritoriously exerted their talents in honour of
this great master. A portion of the valuable details,
which they have preserved from oblivion, has contributed

to our means of establishing this important truth, that the
*domestic style* cannot create a higher feeling for the Fine
Arts in England, or in any country where painting is excluded from the churches, than that which is purely pleasurable, arising from the delightful emotions of a kindred
circle, or from the works of genius, as a refined embellishment of private mansions. This is the utmost effect
which can be produced upon the public mind by the domestic style, however admirable in its productions, and
richly deserving all its honours and lucrative emoluments
in this country, where it was, in the middle of the last
century, and where it is, at present, carried to the highest
excellence.

· It is true that the portraits of great and good men, -
when set up as honorary testimonials in public buildings,
have a strong effect on the minds and manners of their
countrymen: they form valuable instruments of excite-
ment, which ought, on all memorable occasions, to be called
into action. But, the magic pencil of Reynolds was employed to convey to posterity, for more than two generations, the portraits of the wisest, greatest, and most
virtuous Englishmen of his age. Yet the facts, which we
have drawn forth and placed in their most important light
before the public, incontrovertibly prove that the inestimable series of his portraits, with those of Gainsborough,
failed altogether to produce a public taste for the works of
British genius, in the highest department of painting, as
an instrument of moral culture or national glory. So
limited was their effect upon the public mind, that they
even failed, as we have already showed, to open the eyes
of men to the grandeur of Wilson's landscapes, or the
magic simplicity of Gainsborough's village groups and
rural scenery. Facts, here again, must supersede un-

meaning compliments. WILSON died an indigent dependent in 1782. Gainsborough did not die until 1788; and during his life-time, with a few exceptions, his landscapes and rustic figures were without purchasers, and their beauties passed over with neglect.

These facts are not noticed here as any derogation from the genius, or the honourable ambition of Reynolds, Gainsborough, Wilson, or Hogarth. They did more than any other artists ever did before, under such peculiar disadvantages. Their glory is not lessened, by their not having had the power to effect an *impossibility*. Nor is this *impossibility* mentioned to cast a reflection on the British nobility and gentry, their contemporaries, who, in every other point of high-minded feeling, in talents, attainments, munificent public spirit and expanded views, may be justly described as the flower and nobility of the civilized world. The IMPOSSIBILITY is noticed here with something like an idolatrous reverence for the four great masters mentioned, and with a British sense of deference for the age in which they flourished: it is stated, as a signal proof of the utter distaste for British historical painting, originally produced by the total overthrow, rooting out, and banishment of painting and sculpture from the churches, and from these islands, above two centuries before the year 1763, when WEST commenced his career, as an historical painter, in London. How far this general distaste and aversion for the exertions of British genius, in the public style, or highest department of the arts, has or has not been lessened or removed, by the gracious patronage of his late Majesty, by the flourishing annual exhibitions of the Royal Academy, and by the patriotic efforts of the British Institution, in the interval between 1764 and 1825, is a solemn question for after consideration.

We now return to the year 1763, when Mr. WEST commenced his professional career, in London, eleven years after the final establishment of Reynolds in this city. WEST exhibited at Spring Gardens, in 1764 and 1765, some small poetical subjects and portraits; but in 1766, he exhibited two historical pictures, *Pylades* and *Orestes*, and the *Continence of Scipio*. The repelling circumstances, which attended the first, are thus narrated by NORTHCOTE, in his *supplement* to the life of Reynolds: " As any thing in history was, at that period, an almost unexampled effort, *this picture became a matter of much surprise*. His house was soon filled with visitors from all quarters, to see it; and those among the highest rank, who were not able to come to his house, to satisfy their curiosity, desired his permission to have it sent to them; nor did they fail, every time it was returned to him, to accompany it with compliments of the highest commendation, on its great merits. But the most wonderful part of the story is, that, notwithstanding all this vast bustle and commendation bestowed upon this justly admired picture, by which Mr. West's servant gained upwards of thirty pounds, for showing it; yet no one mortal *ever asked the price of the work*, or so much as *offered to give him a commission to paint another subject*." (Supplement, xlii.) This picture was afterwards returned from the exhibition in Spring Gardens, *unsold!* In 1767, West exhibited, Pyrrhus, when a child, brought to Glaucus, King of Illyria, for protection; and four other historical subjects. Dr. Drummond, Archbishop of York, was so struck by the merits of the Pyrrhus, that he gave the young painter a commission to paint the landing of Agrippina, with the ashes of Germanicus, at Brundusium. The profound sentiment, the historical truth and grandeur of this picture, when finished, made so powerful an impression upon the archbishop, that he mentioned it with patriotic exultation to the King, as a triumph of the British pencil over anti-contemporarian and anti-British prejudice. His Majesty signified his pleasure to see the picture and the painter. The interview, which took place in Feb. 1768, not only decided the fortune of WEST, but had a more important influence, in advancing the Fine Arts, in this country, than any circumstance that had ever before occurred in England.

If Mr. West had produced the finest fancy picture in the world, it is very probable, that the King would have been pleased with the imagination displayed in the inven-tion, the taste in the disposition, and the power of the execution: but no more. It would be vain to expect the same effect from the Idylls of *Theocritus,* the elegies of *Tibullus,* or the sonnets of *Petrarch,* as from the *Iliad* of *Homer,* or the Paradise Lost of *Milton.* If VIRGIL had written only his Georgics and Eclogues, he would not now rank as one of the three greatest poets in the world. A fancy picture, however exquisite in taste or execution, can only fulfil its end, that of delighting the fancy, or touch-ing the domestic sensibilities.

If Greece had produced no other poetry but the tra-gedies of Sophocles and Euripides, the odes of Anacreon and Sappho, that country would not have been immortalized by the paintings of Apelles, whose fame has survived their existence, or by the sculpture of Phidias, which still excites the admiration of the world. It requires the highest powers of genius, employed on the highest class of subjects, and applied to the most powerful *living interests,* to pro-duce the highest moral influence on society. But we must not set a Hercules to play at china taws, and then express our wonder that he does not put forth his strength. If

Homer had only written the Battle of the Frogs and Mice, and the Hymns attributed to him, his name would never have reached posterity. His lofty imagination ascended to the highest sublimity and beauty in his personification of the heathen divinities in the Iliad, and the Grecian painters and sculptors formed the Jupiter, the Neptune and Apollo, the Juno, the Venus, Minerva, and all the the other gods and goddesses, with their different characteristics of Homeric sublimity and beauty. The poet imbued his deities with the gross passions of mortals, and elevated his heroes, by conferring upon them super-human powers, and the grand ideal forms of celestials. If the envious carpings of his critics have blamed him for bringing down his gods from heaven, they cannot deny that he has exalted his warriors above the earth. But all this imaginative power would have failed to impress a sublime character upon his poem, or to affect mankind to the end of time, if he had employed his deities and heroes, on subjects foreign from the national pride, and dissevered from the *living interests* of his country. He chose for his subject a memorable war of Greece, signalized by the wisdom of her sages, the valour and victories of her kings and heroes, and the awful interference of her conflicting deities. A subject so national, so heroic and elevated by the alternations of divine wrath and favour, was knit into the heart of every Greek: it fired him with the love of country, and inflamed him with a pious reverence for the ministers of religion and the gods: it formed the very soul of all his *living interests*, and of all the living interests of the state. Here we have the true source and the great end of the epic style in poetry, and of the grand style in painting and sculpture.'

In the Iliad, we have a mighty power of genius, employing the religion of the country, and the national pride, as its

F

moral engines, successfully directed to the mighty purpose
which formed the mind, the manners, and imitative arts of
Greece. It was this divine poem which inspired that great
and glorious people with their love of liberty, and conferred upon them their pre-eminence in arts and arms. It
was the enthusiastic national pride, excited by the lyre of
Homer, that offered up the holy sacrifice of self-devoted
patriots at Thermopylæ, and that triumphed over Persia
at Marathon, Salamis, Platæa, and Mycale. The influence
of that divine poem did not expire with the conquerors of
Xerxes. The glory of their arts did not perish with their
liberties. The spirit of Homer, the ruins of their ancient
temples and sculpture, the genius of their ancient artists,
surviving in sublime and melancholy grandeur, forms the
spirit of the Greeks at this day. It is this spirit which has
roused them to their present heroic struggle, and which
animates every generous breast in the civilized world in
their behalf. Could Homer ever have obtained this mighty
influence if he had been compelled by the fashion of the
day to crowd his Iliad into a dozen pages? Could *Michael
Angelo,* or *Raffaelle,* have worked all the wonders of the
Vatican in a private apartment? We need not any further
argument to show that the country, which would excel in
this style of poetry, painting and sculpture, must employ the
Fine Arts to decorate her churches with the noblest subjects of sacred history, and her other principal public buildings with representations of great national events. She
must do all this, besides laudably calling forth genius to
furnish the splendid apartments of private persons with
elegant embellishments. We are of opinion, that any
discouragement or abandonment of the *domestic style,*
would *not create a power in favour of the public style,* and
must prove a diminution of the national glory. We rejoice

that the British School stands far above all contemporary art, and unequalled by the best of·the old Dutch and Flemish schools, in the domestic style. We would rather stimulate our countrymen to foster fresh excellence in this style, than abate their admiration of the chief artists in this tasteful and agreeable department. We have lamented the unjustifiable attempts to decry the domestic style, with the narrow hope of, thereby, creating a taste for the *public style*, in this country. We rejoice that these injudicious attempts have wholly failed, as they deserved to fail. The domestic style will ever be hallowed, in its proper sphere, by the refinements of social taste and the force of the kindred affections.

We are of opinion that no country or state in the world contains within itself so rich a fund of intellectual and physical means for advancing the two styles, the domestic and public, to their highest point of excellence, as the British empire. Their inestimable resources have been hitherto only kept down by the *church exclusion* of pictures. Let the State remove or counteract the evil, and the triumph of the British School will be completed.

Of the moral effect produced by the grandeur and sentiment of elevated historical pictures, in contradistinction from those subjects which are addressed to the EYE only, there is not, by any means, a just distinction sufficiently impressed upon the public mind. We apply the term and praise of historical painting to a number of pictures in the annual exhibitions, which belong to a different class. This sort of erroneous classification paralyses exertion, and tends to deceive the public into a notion of a British historical school, now flourishing in this country, when that school is on the very verge of extinction! Sir Joshua Reynolds, after having described the great style of true history

painting, proceeds, in his Third Discourse, to enumerate the
class of subjects which are not historical. The weight of
his authority on this important point is a sufficient reason
for here inserting it :—"As for the various departments of
painting, which do not presume to *make such high pretensions, they are many.* None of them are without
their merit, though none enter into competition with this
universal presiding idea of the art. The painters who
have applied themselves more particularly to low and vulgar
characters, and who express with precision the various
shades of passion, as they are exhibited by vulgar minds
(such as we see in the works of Hogarth), deserve great
praise; but as their genius has been employed on low and
confined subjects, the praise which we give must be as
limited as its object. The Merry-making or Quarrelling of
the Boors of Teniers; the same sort of productions of
Brouwer, or Ostade, are excellent in their kind; and the
excellence and its praise will be in proportion, as, in those
limited subjects and peculiar forms, they introduce more
or less of the expression of those passions, as they appear
in general and more enlarged nature. This principle may
be applied to the Battle-pieces of Borgognone, the French
Gallantries of Watteau, and even beyond the exhibition of
animal life, to the Landscapes of Claude Lorraine, and the
Sea Views of Vandervelde. All these painters have, in general, the same right, in different degrees, to the name of a
painter, which a satirist, an epigrammatist, a sonneteer, a
writer of pastorals, or descriptive poetry, has to that of a
poet."

We admire the general candour and correctness of this
classification; although we think Hogarth by far too lightly
mentioned; and we regret that this divisional order has
been overlooked or forgotten since the decease of the great

master whose precepts can never be too much valued nor studied. An inattention to this classification has done much mischief, by mis-directing the public mind, and deceiving many artists. While the public style of history painting has been almost wholly neglected and unpatronized, our honest self-love and commendable national pride have unconsciously led us into the flattering notion that we were encouraging the public style, or highest department of the arts. We have conceived that all was accomplished, when, in reality, we were only multiplying proofs of British superiority in the agreeable, the pleasurable and ornamental branches of the *domestic style*. The admirable productions of the British pencil, in the domestic style, have triumphantly proved that British genius is fully competent to vie with the "great masters of the renowned ages" in the *public style*, if duly patronized.

We have showed that the late King, from 1760 to 1768, had seen all the finest works of Reynolds, Gainsborough, and Wilson, and the whole force of the one hundred and forty-one artists of "*The Incorporated Society*." His Majesty had viewed all these, without having been moved to give a commission to any one of the three great British masters. The whole force of the *domestic style*, in its youthful freshness and glory, annually failed, during those eight years, to induce the royal amateur to take an active part in favour of the British School. We stand here upon the impregnable ground of facts. His majesty had also seen, in the royal palaces, and in the collections of the nobility, a number of fine historical pictures, by the most celebrated old masters. The cartoons of *Raphael* had been under his eye from his childhood, and were then in his possession. These fine works of the great old masters were esteemed and highly valued by the King, but they were valued as the interests of a past age, and of a foreign nation, embarked on the distant ocean of time. In their productions neither the British sovereign nor his people had any share; their glories belonged to generations in the dust, and to another country. They were destitute of a *living interest* for the royal breast, for the British nobility, and for the British nation. We speak here of human nature, such as man is to be found every where. In the same manner, the glories of the *Capella Sistina* were admired at Rome, while painting and sculpture, as we have men_tioned, declined and sunk in the Eternal City.

But the effect upon the King's mind, on viewing WEST's picture of Agrippina landing with the ashes of her husband Germanicus, at Brundusium, corresponded with the dignity of the story; and, as the performance of a British subject, a *grand historical composition* by a BRITISH PENCIL, it made its appeal, at once, to the public spirit and LIVING INTERESTS in the royal breast. The story was well calculated to impress his mind with all the memorable associations connected with the august destinies of the mightiest empire in the ancient world. His Majesty became an immediate party in the fate of a great prince, equally celebrated for his public and private virtues, as a son, a husband and father, a subject, a great commander, and a protector of his people. A recollection of his victories, his learning, his love of the arts, and the tragical death with which the barbarous envy of a tyrant terminated his heroic achievements in the very prime of his life, are so intimately connected with an understanding of the story, that no event could have been been more happily selected to produce a powerful first impression upon the young monarch of a free people. It is a recorded fact, that the King expressed his deep feeling to the Queen, the Archbishop of York, and to Mr. West. He was struck by the power of that art, and by the genius of the artist, which brought before his eyes, with all the "pomp, pride and circumstance" of reality, so signal an event, at the end of seventeen hundred years. The King's satisfaction was extreme. His taste and judgment, as an admirer of the arts, and his pride as a patriot King, were equally gratified. The painter stood before him, a young British subject, in the twenty-ninth year of his age, the first British subject who had ever completely triumphed over the anti-British and anti-contemporarian prejudices of the Continent, by producing a grand historical composition, uniting the learning and judgment of the schools, with the genius of a young enthusiast devoted to that high department of the arts. The story was precisely of that class which Sir Joshua Reynolds has, in his Fourth Discourse, described as belonging to the grand style, and requiring the highest powers of invention.—" With respect to the choice, no subject can be proper that is not generally interesting. It ought to be either some eminent instance of heroic action or heroic suffering. There must be something either in the action, or in the object, in which men are universally concerned, and which powerfully strikes upon the public sympathy."—(Vol. i. p. 80.)

We here, again repeat, that we stand upon the strong ground of facts. The effect of West's *Agrippina* upon the King's mind was not merely productive of praise, of a gracious compliment, and as gracious a dismissal:—the King expressed a desire to take history painting under his special protection and patronage. His Majesty honoured Mr. West with a commission to paint the grand historical subject of Regulus taking leave of the Roman Senate preparatory to his return to Carthage, a devoted sacrifice

for his country. This picture was designed to be conspicuously placed in one of the royal palaces; and it was the
first commission to paint an historical picture, for a royal
palace, given by a British king to a British historical
painter, during many hundred years before.

Thus the commencement of a memorable re-union took
place between two long divided national interests, if the
term may be applied to the Monarchy and the Fine Arts:
the paternal pride, the good taste, and public spirit of
George the Third; the historical works and the genius of
WEST, indisputably formed the golden links of this most
fortunate reconciliation.

The national effect was rapidly conspicuous in the establishment of the Royal Academy, towards the close of 1768,
a few months after this memorable reconciliation. This
unexpected revolution was wrought by the influence, and
under the patronage of the King. *Sir Joshua Reynolds*
has expressly stated, from his own fruitless efforts, and the
many failures of others, the "IMPOSSIBILITY" of
founding that institution, "*but by* THE INFLUENCE
OF MAJESTY." He added, "But there have been
times, when even the influence of Majesty would have been
ineffectual." (See First Discourse). It is certain that the
AGRIPPINA by WEST, a picture, which at once placed
England far beyond all contemporary history painting on
the Continent, and was unequalled by any of the great masters of Italy for two hundred years, was the immediate
cause of this royal patronage, after all the power of the
*domestic style*, in its glory, had failed. WEST'S personal
interviews with his royal patron, when submitting his
sketches for the Regulus to his Majesty's inspection, enabled him to second the strong impression in favour of the
Fine Arts produced by the Agrippina. In one of these in-

terviews he laid the plan for the Royal Academy before the King, for his gracious advice and sanction. VOLTAIRE has remarked, that the history of a public man is, in certain seasons, the history of the time in which he flourished; and his movements, although apparently in the ordinary course, are so frequently connected with public changes, that to omit the one in any public record, is to conceal the real cause of the other. The force of this sound observation applies directly to some parts of MR. WEST's professional career at this period, and to the important influence which his works and his conduct have had in the advancement of the British School. We do not mention these facts as a compliment to his memory, but as circumstances essentially necessary for a true understanding of the present imminent danger to the highest department of the arts. We advert to a particular instance of Mr. West's disinterestedness, which had an immediate effect in the professional elevation of his great contemporary Reynolds, and also in the national restoration of painting and sculpture in England, in 1768.

The associated artists, from 1760 to 1768, in their elections of a president, had uniformly passed by Reynolds, and chosen very inferior artists to fill their chair, although the unrivalled beauty of that great master's portraits had formed a principal attraction in their exhibitions. His professional brethren had thus set an example to the King for passing over Reynolds, in the appointment of a president to the Royal Academy. Their several elections plainly implied that Reynolds, who conferred honour on the association, and dignity on their profession, was not acceptable to them. This was more unaccountable, because he was on their roll as one of their original members. When they elected GEORGE LAMBERT and FRANCIS

HAYMAN their president and vice-president, they had
only appointed Reynolds to the subordinate office of one
of their directors, with a number of artists of noisy pretensions but little capacity. Disgusted at this undeserved
treatment, Reynolds never acted with the *directory*; he
had "long withdrawn himself from the meetings of the association, and had declared publicly that he was *no friend to
their proceedings.*" (Northcote's Mem. of Sir J. R. p. 97.)
From 1752, he had been a constant resident in London,
excepting on short visits to particular friends; but, in
September 1768, when the associated artists were in the
height of their divisions, he manifested his determination
to avoid all co-operation with them, by taking a journey to
Paris with Mr. William Burke; from whence, on the 10th
of November, the latter wrote, stating that he and Reynolds were there, and proposed to return in a few days.—
(Northcote's Memoirs of Sir J. R. p. 98.)    After his return,
Reynolds refused his signature to the proceedings of either
party, and declared his resolution not to act with them.—
(*Ib.* p. 100, and Strange's Inquiry, p. 99.)    Farrington
confirms the fact of the neutrality which Reynolds, on
account of the inconsistency of the association, observed
at this crisis; and he also alludes to the opportunities
which Mr. West enjoyed, of obtaining the influence and
sanction of the king: "Although he (Reynolds) *left* to
*others*, who *were better situated*, the more *active* part of
*planning and proposing to his Majesty the establishment
of a Royal Academy*, he still highly approved the measure."
—"Happily *there were artists* among the seceding members, who, in the situations in which they were placed, had
*opportunity to state their sentiments to his Majesty.*"—(*Ib.*
54.)    These were WEST and Chambers: and the latter,
unwilling to run the hazard of opening a proposition to the

King, declined the task, which Mr. West executed without delay, with the happiest results. The associated artists had just then added to their gross ingratitude, and widened the breach with Reynolds, by electing for their president Joshua Kirby, a teacher of perspective! There was, therefore, not the slightest prospect that, if left to themselves, they would have elected Reynolds.

These repeated elections of Lambert, Hayman and Kirby, had set an example to the King, of nominating an artist free from their objections. As West was honoured with the King's patronage and personal favour, and as his Continence of Scipio, his Pylades and Orestes, Young Pyrrhus, and Agrippina, were in the highest department of painting, and were, confessedly, superior to any historical pictures since the schools of the Caracci, all the artists expected that Mr. West would have been elected president. But Mr. West, who was then only in his twenty-ninth year, diffident of his own claims, and conscious of the anti-historical spirit of the age, with great modesty exerted his influence to procure the election of Reynolds, and to have his election confirmed by the King, although his Majesty had never honoured that great master of grace and harmony with an interview, had never purchased a picture by his hand, nor given employment to his pencil.

Thus George the Third, in 1768, the eighth year of his reign, with a paternal zeal for the improvement and honour of the empire, auspiciously commenced the restoration of those arts which had been crushed by the exclusion of painting and sculpture from the churches, in the reign of Edward VI., Elizabeth, and their successors.

The first salutary effects of this royal and national institution, were experienced by the students. Reynolds, when thus raised to the rank of president of the Royal Academy,

was sensible, that being in that dignified office, as the head
of a national institution, he had new duties to perform, and
a character to sustain, not only in the opinion of England,
but of Europe. He had, when Dr. Johnson was writing
the Idler, in 1759, contributed three papers to that publication. Malone mentions them as our author's first performances, and with them had begun and terminated his
communications with the periodical press. He was then
so sensible of the anti-historical spirit of the age, produced
by the church exclusion of painting, that he abstained from
any attempt in those three papers to reason against it.
During the next ten years, from 1759 to 1769, he had not
resumed the pen, nor had he delivered any lecture or discourse to the associated artists or students at their meetings. Fortunately for the arts, for his own fame, and for
the honour of his country, his elevation to the president's
chair suggested to him, for the first time, the idea of de-
livering a discourse or lecture to the students of the Royal
Academy, and those immortal precepts owe their existence
to the powerful impression produced upon the King's mind
by the *Agrippina* of WEST, the first historical picture in
the grand style which had ever been painted by a British
artist. The personal favor with which his Majesty was graciously pleased to honour WEST, from a view of that noble
composition, and the commission to paint the Regulus, enabled him, as we have already noticed, to obtain the royal
sanction for the plan of the Royal Academy, and for the
election of Reynolds to the chair of president.

Here, again, we are solicitous to show the high power of
history painting, not anxious to pay merited or unmerited
compliments to Mr. West, who probably never foresaw that
the president would deliver discourses to the students.
*Malone* mentions—" the æra of *the establishment of that*

*Academy, which gave rise to the following Discourses."*—
*Reynolds,* himself, with that candour, which formed so
admirable a feature in his character, confirms the fact.—
" If prizes were to be given, it appeared not only proper, but
almost indispensably necessary, that something should be
said by the president on the delivery of those prizes; and
the president for his own credit, would wish to say something more than mere words of compliment; which, by
being frequently repeated, would soon become flat and
uninteresting, and by being uttered to many, would at last
become a distinction to none. I thought, therefore, if I were
to preface this compliment with some instructive observations on the art, when we crowned merit in the artists
whom we rewarded, I might do something to animate and
guide them in their future attempts." *Malone* adds, "Such
was the laudable motive which produced the fifteen Discourses, pronounced by our author between the 2d of Jan.
1769, and the 10th of Dec. 1790, a work which contains
such a body of just criticism on an extremely difficult subject, clothed in such perspicuous, elegant, and nervous language, that it is no exaggerated panegyric to assert that
it will last as long as the English tongue, and contribute no
less than the productions of his pencil, to render his name
immortal." (Some account of SIR JOSHUA REYNOLDS, xi.)

It is perfectly clear, from the evidence of Malone, and
from Sir Joshua Reynolds' own statement, that if the body
of the artists who had, for eight years before, elected *Lambert, Hayman,* and *Kirby,* to fill the chair, had been left
without the advice of *West,* to elect a president of the Royal
Academy, they would have again repeated their gross folly,
by the re-election of one of their former choice; and the
world would not have been enriched by those invaluable Dis-

courses, which have been so often translated on the Continent, and received with universal approbation.

His Majesty, in 1768, and 1769, and thence forward, publicly proved his earnest desire to excite his subjects to patronize the highest department of the FINE ARTS, by setting the nobility and gentry a munificent example in his own person. No efforts could be more earnest or paternal. As far as the king of a free people could exert his influence, the royal wish to lead the public to the great object which he had in mind, was manifested by the frequent admission of Mr. West to the honour of his private conversations, by projecting a magnificent succession of elevated works, to give full scope to his genius, and to exhibit painting in her noblest point of view, and most exalted function. If the long existing prejudice against British painting, in its highest department, produced by the exclusion of pictures from churches, had not retained an entire dominion over the minds of all orders of men, the royal solicitude would have been, to some degree, successful, in causing a few noblemen or gentlemen to give commissions for historical pictures, to WEST and REYNOLDS. But it is a most remarkable fact, that not an instance of the kind occurred until some years afterwards.

. The royal commission in Feb. 1768, to paint the story of Regulus, was followed, on the happy conclusion of that grand composition, by the royal commission to paint *Hamilcar* causing his son Hannibal to swear perpetual hostility against the Romans. The Hannibal having even exceeded the king's sanguine expectations, his majesty signified his pleasure to Mr. West, to paint a succession of striking subjects from ancient history, for all the vacant spaces on the walls of the same apartment in the palace.

A gracious order to decorate Windsor Castle with
representations of signal events from English history, in the
reign of Edward III. was succeeded by a still more comprehensive and magnificent idea. His majesty determined.
to build a royal chapel in the Horns Court, at Windsor
Castle, and to employ WEST to occupy the walls with a
sublime series of sacred subjects, from the Four Dispensations of the revealed law. This was to have been the
triumph of his majesty, as the royal restorer and patron of
the *public style* in the British empire: it was, also, to have
been the signal triumph of British genius, and of WEST
in the highest department of painting, over all our foreign
competitors on the Continent, who had affected to despise
the English as a people disqualified by nature, for the
attainment of excellence in the fine arts.

His Majesty expressed, in due course, his royal wish and
intention, with the most conscientious regard for the purity
of the Established Church, to open the only great field from
whence historical painting had ever emanated in any age
or country, by introducing the practice of illustrating the
interior of the churches in England with paintings from
sacred history. This most important revolution in favour
of the arts, is fully reported by Mr. Galt, in his Life of Mr.
West, and from that interesting work we insert the following passage: " Mr. West, agreeably to the king's desire,
drew up a series of subjects from the Scriptures, which
might represent the important scenes of the Four Dispensations, in such a manner, as the most scrupulous of any sect
or denomination would not justly consider offensive to their
particular sentiments. A day was fixed by His Majesty to
discuss the propriety of the proceeding. Dr. Hurd, afterwards Bishop of Worcester; Dr. Douglas, Bishop of Salis-
bury; the Dean of Windsor, and several other dignitaries,

were present. The King frankly stated his views; at the
same time observing, that he should consider it the greatest
glory of his reign, to have the churches of Britain adorned
with the instructive sublimities of the arts of peace. 'But
when I reflect,' said his Majesty, 'how the ornaments of
art were condemned at the Reformation, and still more
recently in the unhappy times of Charles the First, I am
anxious to govern my own wishes, not only by what is right,
but by what is prudent in this matter. If it is conceived
that I am tacitly bound, as Head of the Church of England,
to prevent any such ornaments from being introduced into
places of worship; or if it be considered at all savouring
in any degree of a popish practice, how decidedly I may
myself think it innocent, I will proceed no further in the
business; but, if the church may be adorned with pictures,
illustrative of great events in the history of religion, as the
Bible itself often is with engravings, I will gladly proceed
with the execution of this design.' On the day specified,
the dignitaries again waited on his Majesty; when Mr.
West had the gratification to hear their decision in favour
of the proposed sublime undertaking. Dr. Hurd reported
the result of their investigation; stating, that they had most
seriously considered the business which his Majesty had
committed to their opinion, and after most mature deliberation, had conscientiously decided, that the introduction
of pictures into the chapel which the king had designed to
erect, could not by any means be the least violation of the
established regulations of the Church of England; and
having attentively examined the list of subjects selected
from the Bible, they were of opinion, that there was not one
of them, which, if properly treated, even a Quaker might
not contemplate with edification."

"The architectural plan of the chapel was afterwards

formed, with the assistance of Mr. West, under the auspices of the King himself, and the chapel was to be ninety feet in length, by fifty in breadth. Mr. Wyatt, the successor of Sir William Chambers, " as the royal architect, was ordered to execute the plan ; and it was designed, that the grand flight of steps in the great staircase should lead to a door opening into the royal closet in the chapel of Revealed Religion." (*Galt's Life of Benjamin West.*)

Mr. West spent a large portion of his life in making designs for this magnificent work, and in meditating upon its several stages. It is known that Lionardo da Vinci, Titian, and other great masters, have each spent years upon a single picture. We are not to be surprised, therefore, that Mr. West, as historical painter to George III. devoted so many years in composing studies and sketches for a series of pictures so well suited to the grandeur of the highest style of painting, to his enthusiastic attachment to his art, and to his religious feelings. It was the object of his professional pride, and the subject of his constant contemplations. Eight of these sublime subjects were finished, and a number of the studies and designs completed ; the plan of the whole was arranged ; when circumstances, which all men lament, occasioned a final laying aside of that great undertaking, to the irreparable loss of the painter, and a fatal stoppage to the advancement of painting in the highest department of the arts.

When the late King did Mr. West the honour to appoint him his historical painter, his Majesty was graciously pleased to accompany that high distinction with an allowance of one thousand pounds a year, which was paid with great punctuality. This liberal grant from the privy purse merely enabled Mr. West to keep his establishment going on, while he was engaged on the magnificent series of

pictures for Windsor Castle, and those from the Four
Dispensations for the intended Chapel Royal. His Majesty always expressed his intention to remunerate Mr.
West in an ample manner in the end, and to honour him
at the close of his labours. Sir Joshua Reynolds was
making from £6,000. to £7,000. a year by portrait painting;
and if Mr. West had adapted his pencil to the taste of the
time, he could have made from two to three thousand a
year by portrait painting. He was frequently urged upon
this point of his own interest; but his enthusiastic attachment to history painting, his gratitude for the honour conferred upon him by his Majesty, and his implicit reliance
upon the royal munificence, induced him to reject all such
friendly suggestions. During upwards of thirty years,
buried in his labours for the King, and only receiving his
pension of £1,000. a year, he had made no provision against
the day of national calamity, which for ever terminated the
beneficent intentions of his royal patron, and covered the
empire with sorrow and consternation.

. This great master was seventy-two years old when
this misfortune occurred. The amount of his annual
allowance had paid him for the pictures he had finished;
but the total stoppage of the work in which he had trea-
sured up all his hopes of fame and fortune, fell with an
oppressive weight upon him at such an advanced age.
He had abstained from the lucrative practice of portrait
painting to execute the King's sublime design; and it
was too late for him to change his hand and seek out new
connections: he had, as it were, to begin the world anew.
and the anti-historical spirit of the time rendered his
prospects in the evening of life clouded and uncertain in
the extreme.

This was, indeed, a heavy blow to the British School,

The sudden overthrow of all Mr. West's professional expectations was, in a public view, an overthrow to the arts, and a loss and discouragement to every British artist. Mr. West's former works were the private property of a very few individuals, and as such were not immediately open to the public. But a magnificent series of sacred subjects on the walls of an edifice dedicated to the worship of God, would have been conspicuously open to the eyes of the world; and would have formed the commencement of the PUBLIC STYLE, under the illustrious House of Brunswick. These pictures, painted by order of the august Head of the Church and State, and hung in the royal chapel in which that monarch performed his devotions, would have gradually fulfilled the royal intentions, by ‖introducing the general practice of church pictures in the British empire, without any fear of a superstitious tendency. In this manner, the sublime and beautiful, the grand materials of *the public style* would have been brought into action as moral instruments, and a source of constant employment, for historical painting would have been created under the revered auspices of the King, the‖ great restorer and patron of the British School, in the eighteenth century.

Thus the exclusion of pictures from churches, the grand obstacle to the great public style of art, in this country, continues to impede the progress of the British School to this day. We therefore quote here the following observations of Sir Joshua Reynolds, that great master of grace, expression, and harmony, who has conferred so much honour on himself and his country, by the admirable productions of his pencil and his immortal Discourses: *"Taking leave of Flanders, we bade adieu at the same time to HISTORY PAINTING. Pictures are no longer the ornament of churches,* and perhaps, *for that reason* ,no longer the ornament of private houses. We naturally acquire *a taste for what we have frequently before our eyes.* No GREAT *historical picture is put up,* which excites the curiosity of the town to see, and tempts the opulent to procure as an ornament to his own house: nothing of this kind being seen, historical paintings are not thought of, and go out of fashion; and the *genius of the country,* which, if room were given it, WOULD EXPAND ITSELF, is *exercised in small curious high finished cabinet pictures."*

...."It is a circumstance to be regretted, by painters at least, that *the Protestant countries* have thought proper to exclude pictures from their churches: how far this circumstance may be the cause THAT NO PROTESTANT COUNTRY *has ever produced a history painter* may be worthy of consideration." "When we separated from the church of Rome, many customs, indifferent in themselves, were considered as wrong, for no other reason, perhaps, but because they were adopted by the communion from which we separated. Among the excesses which this sentiment produced, may be reckoned, the impolitic exclusion of all ornaments from our churches. The violence and acrimony with which the separation was made being now at an end, *it is high time* to assume that reason of which our zeal seemed to have bereaved us. Why religion should not appear pleasing and amiable in its appendages;—why the house of God should not appear as well ornamented and as costly as any private house made for man, no good reason I believe can be assigned. This truth is acknowledged in regard to the external building in Protestant as well as in Roman Catholic countries: churches are always the most magnificent edifices in every city; and why the inside should not

*correspond with its exterior, in this, and every other Pro-*
*testant* country, it would be difficult for Protestants to
state any reasonable cause.

"Many other causes have been assigned why *history*
*painting* has never flourished in this country: but with
such a reason at hand we need not look farther. Let there
be buyers, who are the true Mæcenases, and we shall soon
see sellers vieing with each other in the variety and excellence of their works." (Journey in Flanders, p. 338, vol. 2.
the Literary Works of Sir Joshua Reynolds, Kt.) On the
above clear testimony from the very highest authority
in painting, it may be difficult to offer any observation
that would not tend to weaken its force. The palpable
fact, that no Protestant country on the Continent has
ever produced an historical painter, owing to the exclusion
of pictures from the churches, is full and decisive. Reynolds, in all his discourses and literary compositions, made
it a rule of professional decorum, not to mention, nor allude
to his professional contemporaries, although he highly esti-
mated their powers. According to this professional delicacy,
he never mentioned Gainsborough, Wilson, or Hogarth in
his Discourses during their lives; but his opinion of the
Continent shews, that England, being a Protestant country,
and having excluded pictures from her churches, must be
contented to see the history painting, produced in this
country by the patronage of the late King, perish unless
speedily supported. We however humbly hope that his
Majesty (whose fine taste and paternal desire for the advancement of the arts have been so signally proved), will
be seconded by the public spirit of his Ministers and the
wisdom of Parliament, in devising some efficacious and
immediate measure to counteract the exclusion of pictures from the churches, and to stop the further flight

of every student of painting from the *public style* in the historical field.

As to the great national obstacle, Sir Joshua, in his opinions, (which we have just now quoted), strictly coincides with BARRY, the historical painter, in his "Inquiry into the real and imaginary Obstructions to the Arts in England." We here insert an extract from this artist's valuable publication; although the truth which it states is mixed up with unworthy terms, in mentioning those departments of painting, in which he was not himself a practitioner. "It will appear, that the accidental circumstance of the change of religion, which happened just at the time we should have set out in the arts, gave us a dislike to the superior and nobler parts; the subjects of Christian story, which might be generally understood and felt, were then prohibited, so that except landscape, portrait, and still life, every thing else was either unintelligible, or uninteresting to the people at large." (Chap. v. p. 64.) Barry was perfectly correct in this important fact, that those branches of the domestic style, "landscape, portrait, and still life," (he might have added, fancy subjects and *profane history* in small) were not included in the prohibition of sacred history; but, although they were not prohibited, and although Edward VI., Elizabeth, and her immediate successors were anxious to patronise them, they perished *through the want of a* PUBLIC STYLE to sustain them, and to diffuse a love for the nobler branches of painting in the nation. Barry's language is coarse and inapplicable to any branch of the arts, but the fact of their erroneous and sinking tendency is undeniably true. He adds, that "the artists were *then* naturally led to practise only the baser and lower branches: the farther they advanced in these, the wider they wandered from the truth and dignity of art." This, we repeat it, must ever be the case, where the uncultivated million are the patrons. The most refined education in every department of learning and science will not communicate a discriminative taste for painting. The perusal of the best rules and precepts only renders men obstinate in mistaking their way, when their *eyes* have not been *educated* in their youth by the view of grand examples of painting and sculpture. DR. JOHNSON, whose chief admiration of Reynolds's pencil was its art of making £6,000. a year, is a proof, that without an *educated eye* in painting, learning and high intellectual powers are but blind guides. DR. GOLDSMITH, with more elegant fancy and fine natural taste as a poet, is another instance of similar ignorance in the fine arts, arising from the circumstance that his mind was educated, while his *eye* remained in untaught darkness with respect to painting and sculpture.

Mr. Shee, whose pen and pencil have done him so much honour, agrees in opinion with Sir Joshua Reynolds and Mr. Barry, and has enforced similar arguments in his *"Rhymes on Art."* Barry presented his eloquent plea to the King and the British nation in 1774. He marked the cause of the evil, *church exclusion;* he pointed out the remedy, *church admission.* Seven years later, Sir Joshua, in 1781, wrote his Tour in Flanders, and pointed out the evil, *church exclusion*, and advised the remedy, *church admission.* Twenty-five years after Reynolds's solemn counsel to the nation, SHEE, with equal eloquence and manliness, sounded the alarm again; once more called the attention of the government and nation to the EVIL, CHURCH EXCLUSION, and again advised what Barry and Reynolds had advised so many years before, CHURCH AD-

·MISSION. That artist, in a noble strain of enthusiasm, roused the British students to redoubled exertions.

"Ye generous Youths! by Nature's bounty graced;
Whose throbbing hearts have heard the call of Taste,
With honest ardour in the lists of Fame,
Risk every hope, and rival every claim.
What though *the age on Art unfriendly lowers!*
And public apathy benumbs her powers;
Though Painting *still deplores her luckless fate,*
SHUT FROM THE CHURCH, AND SLIGHTED BY
   THE STATE; ¶
Denied each nobler theme the soul that fires,
That pious zeal, or patriot pride inspires;
Though Fortune's self with Fame confederate flies,
To crown th' o'ervalued skill of foreign skies;
Still undismay'd, let Hope her light impart,
And bold Ambition brave the ills of art."

In 1805, when this able and patriotic advocate for the highest department of painting thus proudly called on the genius of his country to emulate the glories of the ancients, and feelingly appealed to the government in its behalf, he was sensible that there then existed a flattering source of hope in the patronage afforded by George the Third to the *public style*, in the person of Mr. West, the president of the Royal Academy, and historical painter to the King. The ardent poet adverted to that important and exemplary source of encouragement, with strong expectations:— "However, as AN EXAMPLE *has been* set by the AUGUST HEAD OF THE CHURCH in HIS MAJESTY'S CHAPEL at *Windsor Castle,* and also in *the chapel at Greenwich Hospital,* without any apparent ill consequence, it is to be hoped that the remains of the conventicle spirit will soon be exhausted. Perhaps the decorations of our religious temples may yet call forth the genius of a *British Raphael* or Michael Angelo." (*Ibid.* note, p. 101.)

The Poet's "*Remonstrance of a Painter*" excited public attention, and contributed, with the labours and advice of West, and the noble example of *Sir John Fleming Leicester*, towards the formation of the British Institution for the promotion of the Fine Arts, or rather for the advancement of history painting. A number of students in the Royal Academy entered the historical field. We cannot here take the liberty of mentioning those deserving artists by name, which is the less necessary, because their names will be found in the catalogues of the annual exhibitions. But after a few years of honourable exertion, they have, perhaps, with a single exception, been compelled to abandon historical painting, and to betake themselves to painting portraits or small fancy pictures, and making designs for booksellers, as a resource from public apathy and neglect. Of these, the two most persevering and distinguished were HILTON and HAYDON. Under the instructions, and after the enthusiastic example of WEST, they made rapid advances in the Royal Academy. Each devoted his powers to the study of the *public style*, upon a great scale; each obtained several prizes from the British Institution;—but how has their professional career ended? Hilton, with the amenity of *Raphael*, with a rich and graceful invention, an eye for colouring, and great vigour of execution, gave up his whole time and mind to his pencil: he painted several grand compositions from sacred history, which obtained him a high reputation, and one of those pictures was purchased by the patriotic body last mentioned. His merits placed him, for a number of years,

I

in a conspicuous rank before the nation; yet he never received a commission to paint an historical picture for any public edifice! He was upwards of sixteen years painting history upon the precarious prospect of chance purchasers, before he was favoured with a *commission* by any British nobleman or gentleman. The first *commission* which he had the good fortune to be honoured with, was in 1818, to paint the EUROPA for SIR JOHN FLE-MING LEICESTER, a patron, whose name can never be mentioned but with esteem and gratitude by the British artists. At this moment, *Hilton*, with all his acknowledged powers, is still a dependent upon the occasional chance sale of his pictures, which are full of poetical graces and charms, and are painted upon a contracted scale, to suit the fashion of the time, for private collections.

HAYDON, with undaunted energies, and the lofty ambition of rivalling the great masters, painted a succession of grand historical pictures, chiefly upon an expanded scale. The depth and force of his colouring gave additional effect to his drawing and design; and his works would have commanded success in any other country but his own. His earnest enthusiasm, his towering hopes, his immeasurable contempt for every department of painting but the public historical style, are fresh in the minds of amateurs and artists. His genius and his power of execution merited patronage and distinction. What has been the result of his intense devotion? After twenty years of successful study and practice of history painting, all the proud hopes of his aspiring nature have terminated in difficulty, in want and debt, in arrest, imprisonment, and the absolute necessity of fleeing from historical painting, as FROM A ROCK OF RUIN, to take refuge in portrait painting, which he had reviled as the strong hold of imbecility and meanness, and in which he is now compelled to paint for his daily bread!

Here then we have at our doors, the consequences of slighting the advice of BARRY, in 1774; of REYNOLDS, in 1781; and of SHEE, in 1805: the young escape in debt, reproach, humiliation, and danger, from historical painting as from a fatal snare or quicksand! WEST, the venerable Founder and Father of British historical painting, dies, and leaves a sublime series of paintings from sacred and profane history, poetry, and original fancy, a great portion of the labours of his long and meritorious life, *unsold*, as the sole inheritance of his children!

In 1810, five years after the formation of the British Institution, this *unfortunate declension of history painting* was foreseen and foretold by *the author* of " *Cursory Thoughts on the present State of the Fine Arts, occasioned by the founding of the Liverpool Academy.*" That writer stated, that—" Every city or town, which contains a townhall, exchange, or edifice for aggregate assemblies, possesses apartments sufficiently spacious for the arrangement of pictures on a large scale, and is, therefore, a theatre for the display of grand historical compositions. Our history is rich in subjects of elevation; ancient history, also, breathes the spirit of patriotism; and a few hundred or thousand pounds, annually, or occasionally, contributed by the town, the corporation, or the county, and paid *to British artists,* would not only reflect honour on the vicinity, but, if the practice became general, would provide something like a permanent employment for the historical artists; elevate the public taste, and ultimately effect every national object of the arts." (Cursory Thoughts, &c. p. 14.)

The same author, in the following passages, freely

expressed his apprehensions, — "Without some such
PUBLIC PERMANENT SOURCE of *employment* for
*sculpture*, and *historical painting* as that which has been
suggested in these observations, it is to be feared that *the
arts must remain stationary, or lose ground.* Academies
may be founded and artists multiplied, but unless a *demand,
an eagerness, a sort of* PUBLIC NECESSITY *be created
for their works,* an evil instead of a good must ensue. The
thorough degradation of art in Italy, was produced by the
increase of artists keeping pace with the failure of employment. The artist, who could not obtain high commissions,
was compelled to undertake low, and trivial fancies; and
where a crowd of hungry rivals scrambled for bread, the
noble emulation of superior excellence, was forgotten in a
sordid mechanical competition of under-working each
other by reduced prices." (P. 28, 29.)

." There are upwards of five hundred names of artists,
in the catalogues of this year's London exhibitions.
Whoever attentively considers their sources of employment, must feel a serious concern at the prospect
of the great majority of that number. Prizes to young
candidates are bestowed with the most commendable
intentions; and those who bestow them are entitled
to the gratitude of the artists, and the thanks of the
country. But, unfortunately, *prizes only create artists,*
they *do not support them.* They too *often afford a day of
triumph,* as a prelude *to a life of disappointment.* The
British School will, no doubt, continue to display great
genius, and frequently genius of the highest kind; but
genius under heavy disadvantages, and often thrown away
upon inferior subjects. It may produce as it has produced,
shining bursts of excellence in *historical painting,* but
the vein of gold will be still mixed with alloy, and the greatest

strength of exertion followed by fits of weakness. These results must be expected from the want of steady encouragement; for, without steady encouragement there can be no steady practice. The mind of an artist cannot attain, nor continue a lofty flight, unless his spirit is sustained by continual employment." (*Ib.* 29.)

"Again and again, it is necessary to repeat, that *historical art never flourished in any country*, in which it did not possess either from *religion* or *public spirit*, a PERMANENT, PUBLIC SOURCE *of employment*, and *liberal encouragement*. *Wherever* it is left to the *chance patronage of individuals*, IT MUST SINK. Sir Joshua Reynolds has truly observed, that 'our taste for the higher excellence *of style* is not natural, but *acquired*,' and we all know that those who have not acquired this taste, very rarely extend their ideas of perfection in a picture beyond the *polished surface of laborious* finishing, or a *supposed exactness of imitation*." (*Ib.* p. 34.)

In 1813, three years after the writer of the "*Cursory Thoughts*" had published his reflections, Mr. Prince Hoare, in his "*Epochs of the Arts*," expressed similar opinions:— "As far as the real and ultimate excellence of painting, sculpture, and architecture is concerned, *every plan, which is not sanctioned by the support of the government, and not conducted by professional guidance, under just regulations, will necessarily be found ineffectual*." (p. 352.) From p. 253 to 257, the same candid and sound reasoner, has an entire chapter "On the employment of Painting and Sculpture in *Public Halls*."

The prospects and interests of the highest department of the British School, are so intimately connected with the fate of West's splendid gallery of historical pictures, that it is a public duty to enter here into some details. The

high reputation of the late President, is supported by all
the evidences which mark the character of a great master.
His works, as we have showed, wrought a revolution in the
royal breast, in favour of historical painting in the *public
style:* they induced George the Third to take the fine
arts under his gracious patronage and protection, with the
great national object of founding a British School, in every
department of painting and sculpture. We have showed
the immediate effects of this revolution in the royal mind,
by his Majesty's founding the Royal Academy, with an
annual grant from the privy purse, so long as that support
was necessary; by the election of Sir Joshua Reynolds to
fill the chair of president, and all the happy consequences
of that great master's imperishable Discourses.

The works of Raphael, the Caracci, Rubens, and other
celebrated painters, formed so many schools of engraving
in their own time. The works of WEST, also, formed a
school of historical engravers in London. The first prints
by British engravers from British historical paintings, were
the line engraving by John Hall, in 1769, from the Young
Pyrrhus; and the mezzotintos by Green, from the *Agrippina*
and *Regulus,* in the same year. These were followed, in
due succession, by a superb series of prints, from his historical paintings, the impressions of which were purchased
with unprecedented avidity upon the Continent, and soon
compelled our envious rivals to abandon the senseless prejudice, that British artists were incapable of attaining to
excellence in painting. WOOLLETT, HALL, and SHARPE,
the three great line engravers of their day, formed their fine
historical style under the direction of West, in engraving
from his works, for Boydell, in the same manner that the
style of the *Bolswerts, Paul Pontius, Vorsterman,* and the
VISSCHERS was formed under the eye of Rubens. In the

matchless engravings of the Death of Wolfe, the Battle of
La Hogue, and the Death of Nelson, England fought her
battles over again, and will continue to fight and conquer
her enemies to the end of time. The fine impressions and
proofs of the Death of Wolfe, and La Hogue, sold for
unexampled prices both in England and all over Europe.
The late Alderman Boydell, in the year 1790, stated, that
the receipts for the Wolfe alone, amounted to £15,000.
The best engravers in Paris and Vienna copied the Wolfe
and La Hogue, another triumph of British genius. Not
only Woollett, Sharpe, and Hall, but Fitler, Stow, Legatt,
Bartolozzi, Strange, Earlom, Watson, Young, Smith, Cook,
Scorodomoff, Michell, Facius, Liart, Cheeseman, Ryder,
Wilkins, James Heath, Charles Heath, and other eminent
engravers, executed a number of fine prints from his pictures, and extended the fame of West and England all
over the world, by the lucrative export of their engravings.
It is a remarkable fact, already noticed, that the first fine line
engraving ever executed by a British artist, after a British
historical painting, was published by Hall, in 1769, from a
painting by West; and the last great historical print, by
a British artist, Christ healing the Sick, was finished by
Charles Heath, in 1824, from the celebrated picture by the
same master. During a period of nearly fifty years, the
most eminent English engravers continued to derive celebrity and income from his inventions.

. The picture of Christ Healing the Sick in the Temple
was purchased from Mr. West by the British Institution,
for £3,150; being more than double the sum ever before
paid to any British painter for a single production of his
pencil. The Empress of Russia paid Sir Joshua Reynolds
£1,500. for his picture of the Infant Hercules strangling the
Serpents, which was the highest price ever received by that

master. The public-spirited attempt of the British Institution to elevate historical painting, by a signal instance of liberal remuneration, cannot be too highly praised, nor too often mentioned; and we are proud to see that their munificent purchase was richly rewarded.

The Exhibition of Christ healing the Sick was opened April 15th, 1811.

| | | | |
|---|---:|---:|---:|
| Forty subscribers to the picture, at 50 guineas each, | £2,100 | 0 | 0 |
| Seven hundred and ten ditto to the print, at 5 guineas each, | 3,727 | 10 | 0 |
| Receipts from admissions and catalogues, arising only from the time the picture was put on exhibition, | 3,956 | 3 | 0 |
| | £9,788 | 13 | 0 |

From the above there is to be deducted about the sum of £400. the probable amount of the exhibition, if Mr. West's picture had not been placed in the gallery, leaving £9,383. 13s.

In 1812, to June 10th, there were 90 additional subscribers to the print, at 5 guineas each, and the exhibition produced from the opening of the gallery that year to June 10th, about £2,000.

Previous to the purchase of Mr. West's picture, the income of the British Institution, derived from the exhibition, had not in any year reached £900. If we add this £472. 10s. for 90 subscribers, and £1,100. for extra receipts from the exhibition, to the preceding sum of £9,383. 13s. we have a gross sum of £10,956. 3s. up to the 10th of June, 1812. We have also been assured, that from June 10th, 1812, to January, 1825, there has been a large sum received by the farther exhibition of the picture, and from additional sub-scribers for the print. It is stated, that the amount of re-ceipts in that period, have more than paid £1,890. to Mr. Charles Heath for engraving the print, and £300. for paper, and printing the impressions. So that we can refer with tolerable certainty to the sum of £10,956. 3s. derived from the purchase of a single production of Mr. West's pencil in the public style.

Our object being here merely to show the public feeling excited by this picture, we have not struck a balance be-tween the sum paid for it and the receipts; that can only be done by those who know the whole amount received. We have not had before us any official account, and our document is continued only to the 10th of June, 1812; but we have received our information from a gentleman, who is pretty confident in his own statement as far as it goes. If he has been deceived, the error on our part is unintentional: we know of no motive which any person could have for misleading him.

We have already showed the powerful revolution wrought in the King's mind in 1768, by WEST'S grand picture of *Agrippina* landing with the Ashes of Germa-nicus at Brundusium; and we have, in 1812, a circum-stance unparalleled in the history of the arts, in any former age or country, (excepting in that of the death of General Wolfe), a sum so important, we repeat it, derived from a single historical picture. We stand here upon the ground of facts; not in the narrow view of deriving any proof of merit in a work of art from pecuniary considerations, or of complimenting the painter on the result, but to show the power which the highest class of painting has over the hu-man mind: The finest fancy picture in the world could not have produced such an effect upon the public, any

K

more than an affecting elegy, or a beautiful descriptive
poem, could produce the same elevation as a noble epic poem
on the mind of the hearers. Well has Sir Joshua Reynolds
observed in his Fourth Discourse—" In the hands of one
man *it* (painting) makes the *highest pretensions*, as *it is addressed to the noblest faculties:* in the hands of another
it is reduced to a mere matter of ornament, and the painter
has but the humble province of furnishing our apartments
with elegance."

The purchase of this grand composition by the British
Institution, at the price of 3,000 guineas, a price never before
or since paid for a modern picture in this country, fully
proves their exalted sense of WEST's great powers, and
their patriotic desire to excite the nation by their munificent example. They bought it with the public-spirited intention that it should form " *the Polar Star* and FOUN-
DATION STONE OF A BRITISH GALLERY."
(See the description of Christ Healing the Sick, sold at the
British Institution). This single purchase is a reply to
those who have blamed that body for not having worked
an *impossibility*; that is, for not having created a taste in
the nation for the public style of history painting. They
set a glorious example, but *how* has it been followed? Did
it induce any church dignitary to embellish his Church with
a British painting from sacred history? No! Did it per-
suade any corporate body to employ the British historical
pencil to decorate its municipal hall? No. Did it tempt
any individual to give WEST a commission for a grand
historical picture? No! Did it move, or at all effect the
great national obstacle, CHURCH EXCLUSION? No!
Were not all the students, whom the directors had encouraged by prizes and applause, obliged (except HILTON) to
flee from historical painting, as from a path to disgrace and

beggary? Yes! Were not the directors, notwithstanding their just determination in their outset, to encourage only the highest department of painting, obliged, in the end, to confer a premium or prize on a *single head* or *fancy figure*, through a want (as we must presume) of historical claimants? We again take our stand upon the strong ground of facts. Is this so, or is it not so? We have been assured that it is, and we believe it is. When the prize, which was intended for *epic poetry* is conferred upon a *sonnet*, what can we infer (entertaining as we do, a sincere respect for the efforts of the directors), but that there is no epic poet in the land, or that a *Petrarch* was the only claimant.

We have shewed that the *great national obstacle, church exclusion*, was pointed out as threatening the shipwreck of historical painting, by *Barry* in 1774, by *Reynolds* in 1781, by *Shee* in 1805, by *the author* of " *Cursory Thoughts on Founding the Liverpool Academy* " in 1810, and by *Prince Hoare* in 1813. That great national obstacle baffled the combined genius of Reynolds, Gainsborough Wilson, and Hogarth, from 1746 to 1768; it baffled the efforts of the late King, and of the Royal Academy from 1768 to the end of his reign. Why then are we to be surprised, that the great national obstacle has also baffled the efforts of the National Institution in favour of the PUBLIC STYLE, from 1805 to 1825? Church exclusion has baffled all those powers for nearly seventy years, and it will continue to neutralize every other endeavour of genius and patriotism to the end of time, unless the power of the state, that power which formerly crushed and rooted out historical painting in its infancy, be employed to foster and reinstate the PUBLIC STYLE in this country.

By the unanimous voice of the Royal Academicians, WEST was annually elected twenty-seven times to fill the high office of President of the Royal Academy of Painting, Sculpture, and Architecture of London. The British artists could give no higher testimony of his distinguished powers than their thus placing him, from year to year, in the dignified public situation of head of the British school. These elections were annually confirmed by the late King, and latterly by his present Majesty, when Prince Regent, and afterwards. Here we have the highest professional proof, if no other existed, of George the Third's correct judgment, when he conferred upon West the title of his historical painter, and employed his pencil on the sublime series of sacred subjects from the Revelations, for the commencement of the public style, in the intended Royal Chapel in Windsor Castle.

Mr. West's painting rooms were, for more than half a century, inspected by all the eminent foreign artists and amateurs who visited London; and the grandeur, variety, and number of his compositions made an extraordinary impression upon their minds. The extent of his genius was also made known all over Europe by the fine series of prints after his historical pictures. We are not to be surprised, therefore, that he was spontaneously elected an honorary member of all the foreign Academies of Painting, Sculpture, and Architecture on the Continent. These elections by the foreign artists and academies, concurring with twenty-seven elections to the highest honour of his profession, by the Royal Academicians of London, have placed upon public record their high sense of his merits, with so full a measure of contemporary and professional testimony, as to silence the carpings of envy at his excellence. No higher possible proof of any artist's superior genius can be adduced, than the general approbation of his professional contemporaries in every part of the world, where the arts are possessed of a national rank and estimation.

The picture of Christ Healing the Sick in the Temple had been originally designed by Mr. West as a present to the Philadelphia Hospital: but the noblemen and gentlemen of the British Institution, unwilling to let so capital a picture, by a British master, be sent out of the country, purchased it, on a condition that the president should have leave to paint a duplicate from it for the fulfilment of his original intention. The arrival of the duplicate in Philadelphia occasioned an extraordinary sensation. A bill was brought into the House of Representatives, by Mr. John Serjeant, and was passed unanimously by the Senate, to exempt the painting from custom-house duty. On that occasion the name of Benjamin West was mentioned in terms of gratitude and enthusiastic regard in both houses; and this production of his pencil caused the passing of an act of the legislature, to admit the import of all works of art into America duty free. A room was built for its exhibition, at an expence of eighteen hundred guineas, and the crowds of visitors exceeded all expectation. It was the first painting from sacred history, in the public style, by a modern pencil, that had ever been seen in Philadelphia. The secretary, in his official letter, observed, " The accommodations we have provided in our young city, for thy painting of Christ in the Temple, are sufficient to demonstrate our high opinion of the artist and his work. No other picture that has ever been seen in the United States could have justified us in going to the expence we have been at, in building the room for it and its furniture." —" The price for seeing thy painting is ten dollars for a full privilege to every subscriber, and 25 cents each time for every other person; and many have appeared in the room three times in two days, who have paid their 75 cents. In the space of two years the receipts of the exhibition not only repaid the expence of the building, but enabled the committee to enlarge the hospital with wards for the reception of thirty additional patients. The enthusiasm excited by this picture was productive of public honours to the painter. His name was enrolled among those of the founders of the hospital; and in the official writ of appointment addressed to him by the secretary, that body expressed, in the warmest terms, their high esteem for his amiable private character, their gratitude for his invaluable gift, and their admiration of his "exalted genius." He was unanimously elected, with exulting applause, a member of the Academy of Painting in Philadelphia, and of the similar institution at New York; the new world and the old thus bearing testimony to the high powers of his pencil.

That candid and zealous friend of the British School, Mr. *Prince Hoare*, has expressed his warm approbation of the munificent public spirit which the directors of the British Institution evinced in purchasing the grand composition of " *Christ Healing the Sick.*" The opinion of this accomplished amateur, is of so much importance on every subject connected with the state of the fine arts, that we insert the following extract with pleasure :—" From *every surmise of deficiency*, the conduct of the Institution, with respect to *the purchase of the historical picture by Mr.* WEST, *stands eminently exempt.* No act of patriotic zeal towards the art can be more perfect, than the remuneration of contemporary merit, *approved* and *established by the suffrages of professional judgment.* All is then done, which the circumstances of the time allow. *Happily for this country*, the *Picture of* ' *Christ Healing the Sick,*'

ASSUMES SO HIGH a RANK in *graphic composition*, as *to fear no future decline from its present just estimation*. The GREAT MASTER OF COMPOSITION, from whose hand it came, *holds a place in this respect amongst* WHATEVER MODERN *or* ANCIENT SCHOOLS *have produced* OF EMINENCE. *Above the sportive, desultory trains of Venetian grouping,* HE RANKS WITH THE MORE CHASTE COMPOSERS *of the* FLORENTINE and LOMBARD SCHOOLS; and *surpassing many, is excelled by few.* The merits of the picture exhibited at the British Gallery, are not new in the artist, NEARLY FIFTY YEARS *of his life have been passed in the production of* WORKS OF SIMILAR *worth*. But had the merit of the work been less, the act of patriotism in the British Institution, would not have been less perfect." (Epochs of the Arts, p. 222.)

Mr. SHEE's warm sense of the directors' correct judgment and public spirit, and his very high-estimate of West, as the *Head of the British School,* and *of all contemporary art in other countries,* are expressed with great candour in the following passage; and the opinion of this sound thinker is of more weight because it has never been lightly delivered to the public :—" In alluding to *the purchase of Mr. West's picture,* this author cannot resist the opportunity of paying his humble tribute of applause to the liberality of the British Institution in this instance. In common, he trusts, with every respectable member of his profession, he is gratified to see so proud a testimony of *public favour* conferred upon THIS GREAT and VENERABLE ARTIST, who STANDS AT THE HEAD, NOT ONLY OF THE ARTS IN THIS COUNTRY, but *who has produced* WORKS WHICH TAKE THE

LEAD OF HIS COMPETITORS IN EVERY
COUNTRY IN EUROPE. The author considers this
act of the Institution not only just and generous towards
the artist, but highly judicious towards the art. It is a
powerful stimulus, applied at a proper time and in a right
place."—(Shee's Commemoration of Reynolds, Part I. page
33; published in 1814.)

To the above just observations, we subjoin a fact, that
though " *Christ Healing the Sick*" was purchased by a
body of the very best amateur judges of Painting and
Sculpture in Europe, on the ground of its being the
grandest composition from sacred history in modern times,
and entitled to class among the eminent *productions of the
old schools*; yet, in the opinion of the most acknowledged
judges, *West* was roused to still greater exertions, and the
manifestation of still higher powers, in his subsequent
grand pictures of " *Christ Rejected*," and " *Death on the
Pale Horse*." We have no hesitation in stating, that we
perfectly agree with this opinion. But we are fortunately
enabled to insert here, the observations of a distinguished
artist on this extraordinary point. The following remarks
are extracted from the Discourse of the present president
of the Royal Academy, SIR THOMAS LAWRENCE,
delivered to the students in that institution, at the last dis-
tribution of the prizes:

" The elevated philosophy of *Sir Joshua Reynolds*, in
these golden precepts, and that illustrious Society of which
he was the centre, combined with his genius, to give a
*dazzling splendour* to his name, which *seemed to leave him
without competitor*; yet *the powers* and *knowledge* of Mr.
WEST, DESERVED NOT THE CONTRAST IN
THEIR PRESENT FORTUNES. At an era when
historical painting was at the lowest ebb, (with the few

exceptions which the claims of the beautiful and the eminent permitted to the pencil of Sir Joshua). Mr. West,
sustained by the benevolent patronage of his late Majesty,
produced a series of compositions from sacred and profane
history, profoundly studied, and executed with the most
facile power, which not only *were superior to any former
productions of English art*, but, FAR SURPASSING
*contemporary merit on the Continent*, were UNE-
QUALLED *at any period below the School* OF THE
CARACCI. The picture of *the Return of Regulus to
Carthage*, preserved with gracious attention in *the palace
of Buckingham House*, and of the Shipwreck of St. Paul, in
the chapel of the Royal Hospital of Greenwich, are examples that may securely be adduced in testimony of the fact."
" Towards the close of an honoured and laborious life, and
when his advanced age might reasonably have deterred
him from exertion, he produced a large and interesting
work (*Christ Healing the Sick*, purchased by the British
Institution), which, meeting with liberal reward, *so forcibly
excited the admiration of the public, as, even by its attraction, to add new means of patronage to the prompt benevo-
lence that secured it.* This was succeeded by others of
*still more arduous subjects*, of *greater magnitude*, and, IF
POSSIBLE, MORE POWERFULLY IMPRESSIVE.
The display of such ASTONISHING ABILITIES in
age (he was employed on them in his 80th year), combined
with the importance of his sacred subject, *gave him celebrity at the close of his life, far greater than he had ever
before enjoyed*, and he became (almost to forgetfulness of
deceased greatness) *the only popular painter of his country.*'
" Yet what slight circumstances may retard the effect usually produced by death, on the fame of the eminent and the
good! It is now more than three years that we have wit-

nessed at his own residence, an exhibition of *the* ACCU-
MULATED LABOURS of this venerable and great
artist, whose *remains were honoured with a public funeral,*
and WHOSE LOSS WAS FELT *as a* NATIONAL
CALAMITY, *totally neglected* and *deserted:* the spacious rooms in which they are arranged, erected in just
respect to a parent's memory, and due attention to the
imagined expectations of the public, as destitute of spectators as the vacant halls of some corporate bodies; and, but
for the possession of other property of known value, threatening to injure the remaining fortunes of the filial love that
raised them. But though unnoticed by the public, THE
GALLERY *of Mr. West remains, Gentlemen,* FOR YOU,
and EXISTS FOR YOUR INSTRUCTION; while the
extent of knowledge that he possessed, and *was so liberal
to convey*—the useful *weight of his opinions in societies of
the highest rank,* the *gentle humanity of his nature, and
that* PARENTAL FONDNESS *with which* YOUTH
and *its young aspirings were* INSTRUCTED and CHE-
RISHED *by him,* will *render his memory sacred to his
friends,* and *endeared to the schools of this Academy, while
respect for worth and for invaluable service* is *encouraged
in them.*"

"For myself, indebted to his friendship for no inconsiderable portion of that service, I can truly say that *I never esti-
mated the comprehensive ability of that* GREAT MAS-
TER *so* HIGHLY, *as when comparing at Rome his labours
in the memory, with many of* THE MOST CELEBRA-
TED COMPOSITIONS THEN BEFORE ME, OF
*the* REVIVERS *of* MODERN ART, and were the revered friend now living to whom my letters were addressed,
*his report would be evidence of that impression.*"

"I hope it is not possible that the nation should long

continue its neglect, and seem to prove by this indifference
THAT THE GENERAL ENTHUSIASM SO
RECENTLY EXCITED by THOSE FINE PRO-
DUCTIONS, and *the respect then shown to their venerable
author,* were but the impulse and fashion of an hour, de-
pendant on the mere convenience of place and distance,
instead of the rational tribute of the judgment, and the
*feeling protection* of an *enlightened* and *just people."*

We regret exceedingly that we have been obliged to
copy the above valuable matter from the very loose and in-
accurate report published in the newspapers, in which so
much of the President's clearness and force of language is
lost. The observations of one of the highest professional
authorities now living, ought to have been correctly preserved. Sir Thomas Lawrence confirms the astonishing
fact, that WEST was roused by the munificent reward of
the British Institution, and by the public admiration of his
*Christ Healing the Sick,* to the display of still greater energies in his two last sublime compositions, although they
were painted on the verge of his eightieth year. The present President places the splendid series of his paintings
from sacred and profane history above all contemporary
art, and unequalled by the great Italian masters since the
school of the Caracci, that is, above all competition for more
than two hundred years, and, of course, ranking among
the great masters of the preceding period. This agrees
with the judgment of Prince Hoare, who ranks him among
the "*Chaste Composers* of the *Florentine and Lombard
Schools."* A comparison with the works of "*the great
masters of the renowned ages,"* is fatal to all false pretensions, but the British empire may justly be proud, that,
even when tried by this test at Rome, the works of the great
founder and father of British historical painting, and of

the public style in this country, rose higher than ever in
the estimation of Sir Thomas Lawrence, who is justly
looked up to as one of the most competent judges, and
certainly the most candid and impartial authority now in
existence.

The present President of the Royal Academy, speaking
with grateful affection of his predecessor, bears just testimony to " the *gentle humanity of his nature,* and that *parental fondness* with which *youth* and *its young aspirings were
instructed and cherished by him.*" What an eulogium
upon Mr. West, as a man, and as the President of a great
national institution! This record of truth does equal
honour to the memory of the deceased, and to the speaker's
goodness of heart. The great master, whose virtues he
has recorded, was of a mild and amiable character, cordial
in his manners, a stranger to envy, and indefatigable in his
endeavours to promote the advancement of the students
in the Royal Academy. He was at all times, ready to confer fair praise on his contemporaries: was irreproachable
in his morals, and esteemed and honoured in all the relations of private life. These circumstances are not now
mentioned with a view to blazon a panegyric on the deceased founder and father of British historical painting;
but to show, that while his acknowledged genius and the
grand series of his composition entitled him to a munificent public support in his profession, there was nothing in
his private life to justify the failure of his hopes produced
by the discouragement of historical painting in this country.
On the contrary, posterity will bear evidence to the important fact, that the private virtues of Mr. West formed an
additional recommendation of his genius to the liberal patronage of the British empire.

SIR THOMAS LAWRENCE mentions with deep

regret and surprise, the desertion of the spacious exhibition rooms built by the filial reverence of his sons, for the
fame of their deceased parent, with an honest reliance on a
liberal support in their laudable efforts to meet the expectations of the public, and confer honour on the memory of an
eminent and good man, and great artist, " *whose loss was
felt as a* NATIONAL CALAMITY." The passage af-
fords so striking an instance of the coldness and indifference
produced by the great national obstacle, the exclusion of
pictures from churches, that we re-insert the short expression of his feelings, to make a more full impression upon
our readers.—" Yet, what slight circumstances may retard
the effect usually produced by death on the fame of the
eminent and good ! It is now more than three years that
we have witnessed at his own residence an exhibition of
THE ACCUMULATED labours of this venerable and
great master, whose remains were honoured with a public
funeral, and *whose loss was felt as a* NATIONAL
CALAMITY, TOTALLY NEGLECTED and DE-
SERTED : the spacious rooms in which they are
arranged, erected in just respect to a parent's memory,
and due attention to the imagined expectations of the
public, as destitute of spectators as the vacant halls of
a corporate body ; and but, for the possession of other
property of known value, threatening to injure the
remaining fortunes of the filial love that raised them."
    It is to avert the threatened extinction of historical
painting in England, and save her from the continued disgrace of abandoning her artists in the highest department
of the arts, that we have spontaneously taken up the pen,
without any personal connection with the family of Mr.
West, or any personal interest in this question. Unhappily, we all know that this is not the first instance of the

desertion to which an historical painter in this country is exposed. The life and death of Barry are notorious instances of this national apathy. We could here enter into some affecting details, but we prefer the authority of a candid and liberal writer, PRINCE HOARE, from whose interesting work we have already quoted.—" Barry had assiduously improved the faculties of no ordinary kind with which heaven had endowed him. His mind was informed by travel, by research into every study which adorns the scholar and strengthens the artist.—He devoted his life to historical, or rather to poetical painting ; and he passed the greater portion of it in difficulty and partial obscurity ; unable to discover any opportunity of employing his talents and acquirements either greatly to his own advantage, or to that of the community. At length by perseverance, by the force of impressive arguments, and attested professional ability, he made his way to the *single undertaking* which forms the important memorial of his name, at the residence of the *Society of Arts.* With the exception of that solitary opportunity of opening the accumulated stores of his mind, his years of life were, for the most part, consumed unprofitably, amidst discontent, indignation, reproach of the neglect which wronged him, and unconquered unproductive devotion to the research of excellence in his art." (Epochs of Art, p. 160.)

The author of " Cursory Thoughts on the present state of the Fine Arts, occasioned by the Founding of the Liverpool Academy," published in 1810, speaks thus of Barry, —" His first publication after his return from Italy, recommended itself to the world, by an old English stamp of manly plainness, and unanswerable reasoning. He had the good fortune to be honoured by the notice and personal friendship or intimacy of many of the nobility, gentry, and most eminent characters in the literary and mercantile world: his moral character was irreproachable; he was a distinguished member of the Royal Academy ; and for thirteen years professor of painting in that institution. That eminent statesman, Burke, the British Demosthenes, was his early patron, and continued to the last his friend. With all these advantages he also enjoyed the very great advantage of being held as an artist in high estimation by the public. And yet, after a life of struggle, disappointment, and poverty, he was compelled to drink off the cup of sorrow and humiliation to its last dregs, and to submit to have his name advertised as an object for a public subscription, in the hope of obtaining for his wants and gray hairs, that shelter which was refused to his merits. Sad indeed must have been the necessity, which wrung from his proud heart an assent to that last deplorable shift of misfortune. But even there the *evil genius* of *British historical painting* pursued him, and he lived just long enough to endure the whole weight of the misfortune, but died too soon to receive a single shilling of the sum subscribed. *Chatterton* in the bloom of youth, escaping from poverty by poison; and Barry, with the broken spirit of age, faltering an assent to the proclamation of his own distress, are spectacles of terror, grief, and indignation, sufficient to extinguish every spark of genius in the British breast." (p. 21, Cursory Thoughts, &c.)

A writer in the Examiner of Jan. 16, 1825, after remarking on the neglect which Barry, West, and Fuseli have experienced, adds—" MR. PROCTER, who gained both prizes for sculpture and painting, was starved to death in an obscure lodging in Clare Market. And Mr. HAYDON, *after devoting twenty years to history*, and having his works applauded by thousands, lost all his plasters, prints, and books of art, was cast into the King's Bench, and has *taken to portrait painting to get his bread.*" There is no friend of genius or of the British School, but must feel afflicted at this additional effect of the great national obstacle, the exclusion of pictures from churches. The powers of this eminent artist were peculiarly calculated for the public style, and his intense devotion and high practical abilities, and professional ambition, were deserving of public patronage. A *" Memoir of Mr. Haydon,"* published in the European Magazine for Nov. 1824, contains the following passage, which shows that HAYDON has been forced by *the great national obstacle, church exclusion,* to quit historical painting conditionally, and now owes tranquillity and ease to *portrait painting,* that line " which he once held in such contempt. *He will* NEVER UNDERTAKE ANOTHER HISTORICAL WORK *unless employed to do so,* for *with history he has scarcely any other association* but BITTERNESS, DEGRADATION, and SORROW. *Flashes of hope brightening only to be obscured, anticipation of success, generated only to be disappointed."* (p. 87.) Here then have closed the splendid prospects, which this eminent artist justly indulged in on his professional outset! For ourselves, in the hour of his failure and calamity, we have no memory for any thing relative to him, but our remembrance of the ardent spirit with which he encountered the difficulties of the high department to which he devoted his genius. We have no recollection but of his enthusiastic efforts, his fine performances, his honourable ambition, and his commendable endeavour to become the head of an historical school. England is indebted to him for his pupil, BEWICK, a student in historical painting, of refined and elegant invention; for CHRISTMASS, another historical student of distinction and for LANDSEER, a painter of animals, with a genius for every style and class of subject, a youth who has been equalled only by a very few of the most celebrated Flemish painters, but, in his present practice, has never been excelled in any age or nation. We may deceive ourselves into a notion of our advances in taste for the highest style of art; but the nation must suffer by our errors. What is the difference between the fate of JOHN BOSSAM, " that most rare English drawer of STORY WORKS," who was compelled to flee from his pencil into the church to escape starvation, in the reign of Edward VI; and the fate of Mr. Haydon, at the end of two hundred and fifty years, in 1823? Each has been necessitated to abandon historical painting (Haydon, only *until commissioned*), by the same national cause, the dislike or indifference to that style, produced by the exclusion of pictures from churches, an obstacle which must continue to operate for five hundred years to come, unless the government will be pleased, in its wisdom, to take efficacious measures for its counteraction.

The late president, WEST, in a discourse delivered on the anniversary of the establishment of the Royal Academy, remarked, " that the encouragement extended to *the genius of a single living artist* in the *higher classes of art,* though it may produce *but one original work, adds more to the celebrity of a people than all the collectors of accumulated foreign productions.*" Without any comment on the latitude of this excellent remark, which was made in a season of extreme discouragement, we venture to say, that any nobleman, gentleman, or corporate body, who now has, or may have, the public spirit and taste to give a commission to paint an historical picture, upon a grand scale, to Mr. Haydon, will do more towards the preservation of British historical painting, than by the introduction of twenty collections of

M

Italian or Flemish pictures into this country. When 'a town is besieged, all the citizens ought to unite in its defence. When British historical painting is threatened with extinction, every true friend of the British School is bound to sacrifice personal feelings and differences to public principles. ; We must never forget, that, although Reynolds, in the prime of his life, and full flow of 6 or £7000. a year, did not venture, from 1746 to 1773, to make a stand against church exclusion, the anti-historical spirit of the age, *Haydon* has heroically sacrificed the prime of his days in a gallant attempt to establish the public style, in opposition to the apathy of the times, and with the fatal examples of *Hussey, Barry,* and *Procter* before him. We reason this on *public grounds* alone, having no personal intimacy nor communication whatever with this eminent artist. But, as a public duty, we are warranted in the impartial assertion, that no other painter, with the exceptions of Barry and West, ever, so far as he has gone, has made a more strenuous and enthusiastic effort to establish the public style of historical painting in this country, than BENJAMIN ROBERT HAYDON.

We are aware, that there are some individuals who conceive that their personal dignity and character for consistency are concerned, in retaining an offended sense ever after they have once taken an offence and manifested an angry feeling: we will not pretend to guide these gentlemen; but, for the interest of the arts, we earnestly implore them to lay aside all personal considerations in the present tottering, or rather sinking, state of historical painting; not through the want of British genius, but solely through the want of public patronage. We must confess, that we cannot boast of that sort of dignified consistency which nurses a difference for years, whether it be well or ill-

fóunded; we think it more just and more consistent with a
good disposition, to bear anger like the flint, to flame out
upon collision, and straight be cold again. In the hour of
fair open battle we could cry out, with the keen appetite of
Macbeth,

" Lay on, MACDUFF!
" And damn'd be he who first cries, Hold! Enough!"

But, after the fight, we could no more retain an angry
feeling than we could retain our hunger after a feast.
We have never mentioned Mr. Haydon's professional
powers but with due respect; we feel a pride in having
done so: we sincerely wish success to his present endeavours, and only lament that it does not rest with our single
voice to give him a commission to paint a sacred subject on
a grand scale for the metropolitan cathedral. If we had
that power, he should have the commission before the sun
goes down, and we have a confident reliance that his pencil
would do honour to himself and to his country.

There has been much well-meant murmuring against the
State; and the charge of illiberal parsimony and inattention to the interests of the British School, has been, we
conceive, unseasonably urged against more than one administration. The following facts will show the accusa-
tion is so far groundless, that, although *all* remains to
be done, to open a field for the public style, we may safely
assert, no government in Europe has expended, within
the last twenty years, so much money to promote the cultivation of the fine arts as the British Government.

In 1805, his late Majesty's government purchased the
TOWNLEY *Marbles* for £20,000. In 1814, the Administration, under his Royal Highness the Prince Regent, paid
£19,000, including the expenses of landing them in
England, for the *Phygalian Marbles*. In 1816, the admi-

nistration, under His Royal Highness, paid £36,000. for the *Elgin Marbles*; and in 1824, his Majesty's ministers purchased the Angerstein collection of paintings, by the old masters, for the sum of £65,000. Here, during the last and present reign, are ample proofs of a paternal desire in the royal breast to obtain for the public the means of acquiring the grand style in painting and sculpture. The nobility and gentry in the two Houses of Parliament, partook of this commendable anxiety to promote the fine arts. From May 1805, to June 1823, in the short space, of eighteen years, a sum of one hundred and forty thousand pounds has been wisely expended by the legislature, at the instance of the crown, on a principle of enlightened policy, for the avowed purpose of adding to the other glories of this great empire, the glory of competing with the ancients in the great style. No reasonable person can for a moment suppose that these treasures of ancient genius were necessary to form a school of landscape painters, or to enable the British artists to vie with the Dutch and Flemish Schools in painting cattle and rustic nature. In genteel conversations, dramatic scenes, subjects from romances and novels, landscapes, cattle, and rustic nature, the British artists are far superior to all contemporary art, and, in good taste, unequalled by the best Dutch and Flemish masters. The ancient sculpture and pictures, so liberally collected by the British government during the last twenty years, will no doubt prove an advantage to every department of the arts; but they were purchased more especially to promote the study of the great historical style, the only style by which this country can ever hope to equal the ancients, or to employ painting and sculpture as moral instruments of public improvement and national glory.

In addition to these inestimable purchases by the government, we have, within these few years, made immense acquisitions. During the French revolution, England obtained the Orleans collection, with several other valuable collections, and a vast number of detached pictures from all parts of the Continent. This island has been for some years in possession of an inestimable treasure in fine paintings by " the great masters of the renowned ages!" She has had the Cartoons of Raphael for nearly two hundred years; and the Elgin Marbles, the works of Phidias, have been opened to the inspection of artists and the public, from Spring, in 1807 (see Report of the Committee, fol. 65).—With all these materials for improvement, with a Royal Academy to instruct, and a British Institution to encourage and reward, and each meritoriously active in the discharge of its duties, we might have reasonably expected, that the great historical or public style, by which the ancients attained to excellence and immortality, would have found patrons, and that a taste for that style would have been, in some degree, diffused. In the examination of the witnesses before the right honourable committee of the House of Commons on the Elgin Marbles, in Feb. 1816, the question was repeatedly put—" Do you think it of *great importance* to *the improvement of art* that *this collection should become the property of the public?"* The answers were all in the affirmative; and the spirit of the questions and answers shows, that the great style of art was the primary object of the committee and of the respondents, and not merely a school of landscape, cattle, familiar life, and elegant domestic embellishment, in which the British artists have already attained to unrivalled excellence.

SIR THOMAS LAWRENCE's candid reply to the

following question put to him by the *Committee* on the *Elgin Marbles*, is decisive on this point. "*In your own particular line*, do you consider them *of high importance*, *as (in)* forming a *National School?* Answer.—"*In a line of art* which I have very seldom practised, but which it is still my wish to do, *I consider they would*, namely, HISTO-RICAL PAINTING. (Report, fol. p. 38.) This is the whole important truth: but as the church exclusion of paintings has walled up the great field of historical paint-ing, *of what use (until the Government opens a gate)* can the Elgin Marbles be in that high department, from which the British students and British painters are excluded, by the non-existence of commissions, the non-existence of employment, and the non-existence of buyers, and a market?

After all the immense acquisitions of these last thirty years, for the advancement of the British School in the highest department of painting, what have been the results in that department? In every branch of the domestic style, where patronage has been duly afforded, the British artists have triumphantly borne away the palm of genius from their competitors; but in the *public style* of history, how is it? Look but a few years back, and behold BOYDELL, MACKLIN, and BOWYER going forth like husbandmen, who scatter their seed upon the rocks, where it only shoots forth in green blades, that perish long before the day of harvest, for want of a soil to nourish it. The various British gal-leries, formed by these enterprising printsellers, passed away without having taken any hold on the public mind, for the church exclusion of pictures had indurated and rendered steril the intellectual soil in which those exer-tions of British genius would otherwise have taken root. NORTHCOTE, the British Caravaggio, whose picture of the Two Princes smothered in the Tower, forty years ago, furnished a hint for the *Shakspeare Gallery*, to Boydell, has long since been forced to yield to the taste of the age; but this veteran artist continues, occasionally, to make vigorous sallies, *without a commission*, into the province of history. His latest effects show that his pencil is still capable of sustaining the high reputation which he obtained in 1787, by his commanding picture of the death of Wat Tyler. Of the historical pictures which he has painted on commission, with a very few exceptions, the entire have been painted for commercial speculators.

The patriotic Directors of the British Institution, with a vigilant attention to the discharge of their duty, have this year purchased one of NORTHCOTE'S latest works, "The Entombing of Christ." In France or Italy, a capital painting like this, by a native artist, would have tempted a competition to possess it; but is it not a melancholy truth, that if the Directors had not wisely made the purchase, it might have remained (thanks to the *church exclusion!* ) for years *unsold* in the artist's apartments?

We have already noticed the dispersion of the historic galleries of *Boydell*, *Macklin*, and *Bowyer*, without their having laid hold upon the public mind, through the want of a soil to take root in. It is well known that the sublime and beautiful flights of imagination in FUSELI'S *Miltonic Gallery* did not rescue that most extraordinary effort of Genius, without a patron or a commission, from a similar fate. We have also remarked, that the young artists who applied themselves to historical painting at the call of the British Institution in 1805, have gradually been obliged, perhaps with the exception of Hilton, to quit history painting, to suit their pencils to the taste of the time, and have fallen into more popular branches of practice. HILTON still acquires fresh laurels in the *poetry* of his art; but he no longer displays his powers on a grand scale, as

the painter of sacred history. HAYDON, a young cham-
pion of the public style, who went forth like a giant, glory-
ing in his strength, in 1808 and 1809, after so many years
of enthusiastic hope and arduous struggle, has been necessitated to take to portrait painting for a livelihood.
The spacious exhibition rooms, containing the magnificent
series of historical paintings by the late President, West,
are wholly deserted by the public. Excepting the few fine
specimens of this class, at the British Institution this year,
we do not hear of any great public picture being now in
hand, either upon a commission, an exhibitional speculation, or the precarious issue of a chance purchaser.

These facts show, that our inestimable acquisitions from
*Greece* and *Italy* have hitherto unhappily failed to open
a field of employment for the historical pencil in the highest
department, or to diffuse a taste for that grand public style
by which the ancients acquired their highest excellence.

Where does the cause of this failure lie? *Not in* his
Majesty—for the fine taste of that illustrious personage,
and his gracious desire to patronise British genius, are
well known and evinced by his munificent purchases of
British pictures for the embellishment of the royal apartments: not in his Majesty's Government, or the Legislature: for the Government and Legislature have been liberal
in amassing fine specimens of painting and sculpture for
the advancement of the British School: not in the country,
for the country has proved itself rich in genius: not in
the Royal Academy, for the Royal Academy has sent forth
a number of students who have reflected honour on its
course of instruction: not in the British Institution, for
that public-spirited body has rewarded merit by prizes, and
by purchase: not in the young historical painters, for they
have exhibited historical pictures upon a grand scale, which

have proved them worthy of employment in the public style, and capable of conferring reputation on the empire. Where his Majesty, the Government, the Legislature, the country, the Royal Academy, the British Institution, the young historical painters, the veterans Northcote and West, the President of the Royal Academy, the venerable founder and father of British historical painting, have all pressed forward, with one noble impulse, to the same national object, what can have occasioned so untoward a conclusion? What—but the old rooted evil, CHURCH EXCLUSION, which nearly seventy years ago defeated the paternal efforts of his late Majesty, and the genius of Reynolds, Gainsborough, Wilson, Hogarth, and the one hundred and one associated artists? Although upon every other ground the best materials have been collected, and the best dispositions existed, CHURCH EXCLUSION, the great kill-genius of the age, neutralized, all in the highest department. After the young candidate for historical fame had gained a prize and sold a picture or two, CHURCH EXCLUSION shut him out from further hope, from further employment and patronage; that appalling power forced him into the withering grasp of discontent, distress and poverty; beat down the bravery of his nature; and left him no prospect but that of flying from the high ground of his hopes, or of sinking, an heart-broken and deserted victim in the very field of his glory.

Let us imagine that the government of a foreign state has erected a vast machinery at a great expense of time, money, and labour, and has invited its people to invest their capital in a manufacture to be carried on by means of this machinery. If, after all, facts prove that there are no buyers in the proposed direction or field, and no market for the goods when fabricated,—what is to be done? Surely

N

if the government possess the power to create a market,
and that the success of the manufacture be essential to the
interests and honour of the state, it would be wiser to open
a mart than to let the machinery lie useless and inactive,.
bringing down on the possessors an imputation of their
being disqualified by nature from turning it to their own
advantage. We may reason from this illustration to present circumstances. All our invaluable purchases of ancient
marbles and paintings for a national gallery, are but the
machinery to enable the British artists to vie with the
ancients, not merely to be their imitators in the highest
style of art. The sculpture of the *Townley*, *Phygalian*,
and *Elgin* collections, and the *Angerstein* paintings, were
purchased only as a means towards the accomplishment of
that great national end. But there are no commissions
given for paintings in the public style, and there are neither churches nor public edifices open to receive them.
There is no market for them. We are not to be surprised,
therefore, if the prospect of neglect, poverty, and imprisonment, is sufficient to terrify every young man of high-
minded feelings, from risking the *capital* of his hopes
and genius in so desperate an undertaking.

From present circumstances it would seem, that all the
elevated examples of design and execution in marble and
canvas, which have been so liberally purchased by Government, and are now amassed in England, were collected for
no other purpose, but to prove that the formation of maga-
zines of the best materials for the erection of an edifice
consecrated to national glory, will neither lay the foundation nor perfect the building, unless the builders who are
to be employed are sure of being rewarded for their labour.
If there be no fund for paying them, and no prospect but
indigence and obscurity for their industry, they will leave

the projected structure to rise miraculously by itself, and will hasten to erect humbler habitations for private individuals, by whom they are sure to be paid for their time and labour. This is the state in the high department of history painting. The British Institution have conferred rewards and prizes in discharge of their duty, but that public-spirited body, although they have done so much good, cannot work impossibilities. The young historical painters have exerted themselves in the outset, so long as there was the least prospect of obtaining a livelihood; but there being no productive field for their exertions, no commissions in the public style, they have found it necessary to accommodate themselves to the taste of the time, and to devote their pencils to the lucrative task of furnishing the private apartments of their patrons with elegant embellishments.

Where then is the remedy? We presume not to offer any thing beyond a very humble suggestion. We discover this remedy in the paternal bosom of our gracious Sovereign, in the wisdom of his Government, and in the liberality of Parliament. That which pulled down, alone has power to re-build. The royal will, under Edward VI. and Elizabeth, crushed the *public* style of history painting, by the exclusion of pictures and statues from churches. The power of the state alone, in 1825, can counteract the effect of church exclusion.

A nation may clothe herself in a robe of honour from Greece, Rome, and the golden days of Leo, but her majestic array will only turn out to her discredit, unless she can show a robe of as rare an invention from the looms of her own people. A rich man, by purchasing a poem, a painting, or a piece of sculpture, cannot acquire the fame of having written, painted, or chiseled the objects of his purchase : nor can a nation acquire any claim to superior genius by having enriched herself with the painting and sculpture of another people. She can only become illustrious in the highest style of those arts by the performances of her native painters and sculptors. She cannot become renowned for excellence in those intellectual refinements by *importing* the admirable productions of foreigners. She may grow rich in foreign collections, and be a loser in reputation, unless her munificent patronage of her native artists, and their improvement in the highest department of art, keep pace with her *importations*. It was not by foreign valour that England won the bloody laurels of Cressy, of Poictiers, and Agincourt. It was not by mercenary aliens she triumphed at Trafalgar. These victories would not shed so bright a lustre on the page of British history if they had not been obtained by British heroism. It is by a national patronage of British genius, by affording a constant encouragement to the British pencil and the British chisel alone, that the British empire can hope to vie with the ancients in painting and sculpture. We can never vie with the old schools so long as the highest department of painting is closed against the exertion of living genius, by the exclusion of pictures from churches and public halls. It is in a NATIONAL GALLERY of BRITISH HISTORICAL PAINTINGS that her great national triumphs in the arts will be accomplished, and that she will lead the way to the cultivation and establishment of the *public style.*

It is a glorious boast for England to possess the *Townley, Phygalian,* and *Elgin Marbles,* the *Cartoons* of *Raphael,* and a *National Gallery of Paintings, by the great masters of the renowned ages!* But if all the fine sculpture and paintings in Italy were transported to the British capital at this moment, and added to our present treasures, the accession would only increase our materials for educating artists in the highest style; it would not add a jot to our means of affording them employment in that department when educated. Unless the importation opened a field for the patronage of the British pencil and chisel in the highest department, it would only *overlay* and *repress the spirit of British genius*, by multiplying the means of invidious comparison between its discouraged and desultory efforts in the *public style*, with the most perfect productions of the celebrated old schools. Unless the Government of this country forms a national gallery of British historical paintings, her national gallery of acquisitions from the ancients, may be converted into a handle by her enemies, for reviving the exploded calumnies of Du Bos, Winkleman, Montesquieu, and Voltaire. Our envious competitors may say, the great authority of the Royal Academy of England has inculcated that "the language of Michael Angelo, is THE LANGUAGE OF THE GODS;" he has exerted his eloquence to urge his countrymen to study "THIS GRAND STYLE OF INVENTION." Nearly forty years have passed since he pressed them to this proof of their taste, this trial of their great historical powers. They have imported a rich treasure of ancient sculpture and painting, as a means of enabling their artists to rival the old schools, and to carry off the palm of genius from all other nations. But where are the results of their first President's eloquence and of their exertions? The few of their artists who have ventured to follow his precepts and to climb the steeps of fame to which he pointed, have been neglected and discouraged in their progress, and finally abandoned as visionary enthusiasts to poverty and disgrace!!!

The *Elgin Marbles* are deservedly admired, and I trust that they will be every day more admired, and better un-

derstood : but many objects are admired and highly prized by
the public without possessing any influence on the national
taste. Men visit and value the tombs of their ancestors, but
cease to think of them in the business of life. The town
crowded lately to an exhibition of ancient armour, but we
have not heard that any of the admirers cased himself in
steel, and marched forth, armed cap-à-pie, to visit his friends.
The spectators for years admired *John Kemble* in the
Roman costume, but they continued to employ the dandy
tailors of Cork-street, to fit them in the newest fashion,
for the dining apartment and ball room. The best Dutch
and Flemish painters travelled to Italy for improvement,
and during their studies there, extolled and admired the
antique statues and the paintings of the great old masters.
But after their return home, with all their admiration of
the *gusto grande* of Italy, they painted familiar life in the
German, Dutch, and Flemish taste. This is not mentioned
as their fault, but as a result of circumstances formed by
the spirit of their country. If *Teniers, Jan Steen, Ostade,*
*Berghem,* and *Wouvermans* had visited Rome, and successfully exchanged their own country manner for the
grand style, they must have resumed the Dutch and
Flemish subjects at the Hague and Amsterdam; for the
grand Italian style and subjects would not have found a
market in Holland and Flanders. We need only instance
the Prince of the Flemish school, that truly great master,
Rubens, as a proof that it is one thing to see, admire, and
praise the masterpieces of the grand style, and another
thing to adopt their purity and elevation as a rule of practice. That whole nations, and schools of eminent painters
and sculptors may fall into this strange inconsistency of
seeing and admiring the grand style, and neglecting to
adopt it, there are quite proofs enough to be found, not only

in the decline, but in the rise of the arts in Italy. Sir.
Joshua Reynolds, in his Fifteenth Discourse, adverts to
this strange circumstance. "It is impossible not to express.
some surprise, that the *race of painters* who preceded Michael Angelo, men of acknowledged great abilities, *should
never have thought of transferring a little of that grandeur.
of outline* which they could *not but see* and *admire in ancient
sculpture, into their own works*; but they appear to have
considered sculpture as the *later schools of artists look at the
inventions of Michael Angelo—as something to be admired,*
but *with which they have nothing to do: quod super nos,
nihil ad nos.* The artists of that age, even Raphael
himself, seemed to be going on contentedly in the dry manner of *Pietro Perugino;* and if *Michael Angelo* had never
appeared, the art might still have continued in the same
style."

These facts show, that if all the wonders of art that ever
existed in Greece or Italy were at this moment in one
national gallery in London, although we are quite sure that
they would be prodigiously extolled and admired, we have
reason to fear that they would have little or no effect upon
the public taste in the grand style, so long as the great
national obstacle, the exclusion of pictures from churches
is opposed to them. That obstacle has formed the spirit
of the age and nation, and it has hitherto mastered every
effort to subdue or mitigate it. The painters who feel impelled to practice in the public style, know by bitter experience, that their performances in that department will
probably be left unsold, and slighted upon their hands; they
are, therefore, necessitated to comply with the times, and
with all their admiration of the Elgin Marbles, and of
Raphael's Cartoons, and the Angerstein collection, they are
compelled to paint such light, agreeable, fancy, or familiar

subjects, as are in demand, and for which they have something like a certainty of finding purchasers. We have already quoted Sir Joshua Reynolds's remark, that " NO PROTESTANT COUNTRY EVER PRODUCED AN HISTORICAL PAINTER," for the palpable reason, that pictures being excluded from churches in Protestant countries, there is no other soil in those states for the PUBLIC STYLE to strike a root in. This it is that has hitherto opposed an *impossibility* to the persevering patriotism of the British Institution. Church exclusion having closed every field in England against the public style, it is quite clear that nothing can be done for it until the Government will be pleased in its wisdom, on broad public grounds, to establish a NATIONAL GALLERY of BRITISH HISTORY PAINTING, and to open a field for the patronage of the public style, by embellishing the interiors of a certain class of public buildings, with historical pictures by *British artists.* Surely to afford forty or fifty thousand pounds in the outset, and an annual fund of a few thousand pounds to enable her artists to vie in the highest excellence of the arts with the ancients, can weigh but as a feather in the expenditure of an empire, which in time of war has raised £60,000,000. in taxes ; has maintained 6 or 700,000 soldiers and seamen in arms ; has subsidised all the great military powers, and comprehends territories in Europe, America, Asia, and Africa, of greater extent, and infinitely greater resources than ever Rome was possessed of at the height of her grandeur.

Until the Government, in its better judgment, will be pleased to adopt some such efficacious measures, experience from 1746 to 1825 proves, that there are at present as few motives for a young British painter to study the *public* style, as there are inducements for a fashionable

London tailor to make up the Roman costume in the time of Coriolanus, or the Grecian garb in the days of Pericles, for his Bond-street customers. Our great consolation in the mean time is this, that the domestic style is introducing fresh candidates for fame to public favour in every exhibition, and every year reaping large increase of honour and reputation for the British school.

That we may not be considered to differ in our view from the most competent authorities in this country, we again refer to the passage in the publication of the British Institution in 1813, in which it is stated that WEST'S picture of " *Christ Healing the Sick*," was purchased " through the generosity of the subscribers, to stand *as the polar star*, or FOUNDATION STONE OF A BRITISH GALLERY." The same important fact is thus mentioned by MR. PRINCE HOARE. — " Finally redeeming the neglect of the age, and OFFERING TO THE STATE *an example of patronage*, the Directors purchased of ONE GREAT HISTORICAL PAINTER one of his *best* and *latest works*, at the *splendid* price of 3,000 guineas; PROPOSING, AT THE SAME TIME, that *it shall form the* COMMENCEMENT OF A GALLERY of the ENGLISH SCHOOL." (Epochs of Art. p. 208.)

We have to add to the above testimony our own knowledge, received from the late President himself, in 1819. " It is the great pride of my mind, to think that my picture of Christ Healing the Sick is to be the commencement of a BRITISH HISTORICAL GALLERY. This assurance from the directors was the greatest gratification to me, when they did me the honour to purchase that picture."

We have here showed that the most public-spirited, enlightened, and dignified amateurs in the empire, deter-

o

mined in favour of a *British historical gallery fourteen years ago*; and that *they then looked to* THE STATE *for the accomplishment of their great national object*. We shall now show that our ideas of the GRAND STYLE, and its elevated objects, as an instrument of moral culture and national glory, are precisely the same as those already promulgated by that distinguished body. " Convinced that the *pre-eminence* which the imitative arts attained in *certain distinguished periods of ancient Greece and modern Italy*, was produced, not by fortuitous circumstances, but BY GREAT AND SPLENDID PATRONAGE; and persuaded that our own countrymen are capable of the same excellence in the arts as they have attained in every branch of science and literature, we *solicit that they may be encouraged to consider those excellent and immortal examples of the Grecian and Italian schools as the objects,* *not merely of* IMITATION, but OF COMPETITION. In a country where native energy is most abundant, we ask that *professional taste and talent, and national patronage*, be *no longer confined to* INFERIOR OBJECTS; but *that our artists may be encouraged to direct their attention to* HIGHER *and* NOBLER ATTAINMENTS;— to *paint the mind and passions of man*, and to ILLUS-TRATE *the* GREAT EVENTS *which have been recorded in the history of the world*."

The above is an extract from the circular letter printed and issued by the original Committee of the British Institution. It will be found, page 23, in their proceedings, published by John Hatchard, Piccadilly, 1805.

At a crisis, when facts show that the PUBLIC STYLE is tottering on the brink of extinction, we may be pardoned for inserting another extract from the same invaluable document.—" And it is in this respect worthy of observation,

that, IF WE DO NOT ADVANCE, WE MUST RE-
CEDE; and that *when* WE CEASE TO IMPROVE,
we *shall begin to* DEGENERATE. These considerations are of increased importance at the present moment,
when it appears to be the object of other powers, to form
great establishments for painting and sculpture, and to
*extend, by the arts of peace, the influence which they have
acquired in war.* We feel, however, no apprehension, but
that the spirit of the British artist will be awakened and
invigorated, *whenever a free and fair scope shall be given
to his talents;*—whenever he shall be stimulated by THE
SAME PATRONAGE as that which *raised and rewarded the Italian and Grecian masters;*—a PATRONAGE,
WITHOUT WHICH, if *we refer to historical evidence,*
we shall find that NO HIGH EXCELLENCE IN ART
HAS EVER BEEN OBTAINED *in* ANY AGE, *or in*
ANY COUNTRY."

We agree most fully in the direct meaning and truth of
the above. Unfortunately, there is no public patronage
whatever in this country for the grand style, which Sir
Joshua Reynolds has designated by the significant statement of a fact—" No GREAT HISTORICAL PIC-
TURE is *put up.*" As the exclusion of pictures from
churches has suppressed all that public source of patronage which raised and supported the Grecian and Italian
artists, we join most earnestly with the reasonable and
manly declaration of the Committee of the British Institution, in their description of that public source, as " a
patronage, without which, if we refer to historical evidence,
we shall find that no high excellence in art has ever been
obtained in any age, or in any country." In the latter part
of the sentence, their meaning evidently seems this;—without which, the highest excellence in art has never been

obtained, and never can be obtained, in any age, or in any
country. History proves the fact, that it was by the highest
source of public patronage alone, that the artists of Greece
and Italy were roused to their immortal performances.

The names which appear to the above important record
are, " Dartmouth, Abercorn, Lowther, Mulgrave, Isaac
Corry, Charles Long, George Beaumont, Abraham Hume,
Francis Baring, R. P. Knight, Thomas Hope, William
Smith, Thomas Bernard," It would be impossible to find
in all Europe, any nine other amateurs, whose rank, talents,
refined taste, and patriotic views entitled them to equal
authority, on any question relative to the advancement of
the fine arts. It is our pride to agree with them, with our
whole heart, in their reasonable and admirable declaration.

We quote again with great delight, the following passage from the catalogue of that public spirited body, the
British Institution, in the year 1811:—" Upon offering
some remarks on the object, plan, and progress of the British Institution, it should be premised, that in *its foundation,* the FINE ARTS have been appreciated, not merely
as sources of revenue, or as means of civil refinement, but
have been *revered and honoured for a* NOBLER and
MORE USEFUL PURPOSE. When directed to
INTELLECTUAL and NATIONAL OBJECTS, and
whilst their character is neither degraded by vulgar subjects, nor sullied by licentious images, they *are calculated
to* RAISE *the* STANDARD *of* MORALITY *and*
PATRIOTISM ; *to attract the homage* and *respect of
foreign nations, and produce those intellectual and virtuous
feelings, which are perpetually alive to the welfare and
glory of the country,* and *prepared to offer every sacrifice,
and to make every exertion in its defence."* " The
governors of the Institution, in directing their attention

towards their object, have not listened to those insinua-
tions which presume a *physical defect* in the natives of the
British Isles. They can discover no reason why British
artists should not excel in the fine arts; or why *the
countrymen of* REYNOLDS and WEST should dread
a competition with *any* modern school."

The illustrious body which thus signalized REYNOLDS
and WEST before all Europe, as the two great luminaries
of the British School, was composed of the first person-
ages in the world. It consisted of their late Majesties, of
his Royal Highness the PRINCE REGENT, and sixteen additional members of the royal family, royal dukes,
and royal duchesses; of thirty-nine British peers, dukes,
marquesses, earls, and viscounts; and the untitled members included a number of gentlemen eminently distinguished for taste, talents, public spirit, and attainments.
To be so conspicuously honoured by this exalted body
must have been highly gratifying to Mr. West in his age.
The high point of view, in which they publicly connected
the names of WEST and REYNOLDS, with the fame of
Britain, was well calculated to raise the British School,
and its two great pillars, in the estimation of other nations.
We have been charged, for some years, with entertaining
romantic and singular views of the high moral and national
end and aim of the fine arts. We have been told that our
views are difficult, and some have added, impracticable;
but we reply, that difficulties are the precious materials
by which men of genius and great nations weave
the web of glory; facilities are the ready-made materials for ordinary minds. We trust that we have now,
once for all, justified ourselves from this charge of singularity, by having showed that the most distinguished association of royal, noble, and dignified amateurs in existence,

was expressly founded for the purpose of elevating painting and sculpture from ordinary aims, " to a *nobler* and
*more useful* purpose," "to *intellectual* and *national
objects;*" "*to raise the standard* of *morality* and *patriotism;*"
" to *attract the homage* and *respect of foreign nations,*"
and to arm the hand of British valour, if necessary, in
defence of the country. We stand so high, and so proudly
connected with the illustrious body, in the concurring end
and aim of our spontaneous writings on this subject for
thirty years, and in the whole train of our independent
thinking for the advancement of the fine arts, that we may
henceforward calmly hear the charge of *singularity* in our
views of the national means for promoting the *public style*,
not only without reply or regret, but with honest pride and
satisfaction.

Here again to show that our opinions are not delivered
with a view to a *temporary object*, or to promote a partial
interest, we insert the following passages from a tract
published in 1810. By those extracts we hope to mark,
with a reiterated force, the distinction between the gene-
rative *cause* or *source* of the public style, and that which is
*domestic* :—

" The million, unless led to look higher, by *some great
counteracting principle*, and *public examples* of *British art
in the superior style*, will *ever be best pleased by representations* of *familiar nature*. They will still eagerly desire
to behold those objects painted, the prototypes of which they
are in the habit of seeing daily. This preference is founded
in their considering themselves best qualified to judge of
such pictures, from the circumstance of possessing, at all
times, in their own eyes, a sure standard to ascertain the
degree of resemblance between the work of the artist and
the original objects in nature."

" A proof of the foregoing reasoning will be found in the instances of *Italy* and *Holland*. In *the former*, THE CHURCHES *afforded* PUBLIC and CONSTANT EXAMPLES *of the superior style of art*, the *daily contemplation of which formed the taste of individuals* and of *the Public*. The *cabinet* and *gallery pictures were, therefore, painted in conformity with the taste of the latter, in* THE SAME SUPERIOR STYLE; and if the patron or employer committed some errors in directing the mode of treatment, still that circumstance was more than balanced by *the elevation* of *his choice*."

" On the contrary, in *Holland*, OWING TO THE WANT OF PUBLIC EXAMPLES *in* THE SUPERIOR STYLE, *to form the taste of the Public*, ART TOOK AN OPPOSITE COURSE. *Painting* being left to support herself by *individual patronage, never rose above the level of ordinary conception*. The *artists were obliged to please the crowd*. Hence, they painted landscapes, cattle, subjects of ordinary and familiar nature, dead game, and still life, suited to the *fancy*, or *uncultivated taste* of *their employers*; and the excellence with which they executed these subjects, often compels us to forget their worst choice."

" It is of the last importance, *in looking to the prospects of British art*, to *mark this leading distinction*. IN ITALY the *painters*, or rather PAINTING, by PUBLIC EXAMPLES, FORMED THE TASTE OF INDIVIDUALS, and THE PUBLIC FOLLOWED ART. In HOLLAND, *individuals formed the taste* and *governed the practice of the painters*; and ART, *instead of leading*, FOLLOWED THE TASTE OF THE PUBLIC.

" As to the silly notion, that the damp and foggy climate

of Holland caused the difference between Dutch and
Italian art, it is not worth an argument. Those who
believe it may. It is the pedantic sophistry by which *Du
Bos, Montesquieu,* and *Winkelman,* endeavoured to discou-
rage the people of this country from *ever attempting any-
thing elevated in the Arts.*" (Cursory Thoughts. p. 34, 35,)
Again we remind our readers, that the above tract was
written and published in 1810.

The directors of the British Institution, in their admirable publications, have distinctly defined the GREAT
MORAL END and INSTRUCTIVE AIM of the
PUBLIC STYLE, which they expressly associated to
promote as their primary object. The above extracts, from
the "Cursory Thoughts," founded in the experience of the
old foreign schools, as clearly show that the *public style
alone* can create an elevated public taste, and form a source
of *public patronage* similar to that "which *raised* and
*rewarded the Italian* and *Grecian Masters;*" (and again,
to borrow the words of the British Institution in 1805) "a
patronage, without which, if we refer to historical evidence,
we shall find that no high excellence in art has ever been
obtained in any age or in any country." The necessity
of opening a public source of patronage, is on all hands
allowed, to counteract the great *National Evil,* the church
exclusion of pictures. The British Institution, in their pre-
liminary notice in 1811, remarked, that their body had
"not attained the magnitude and importance, which in
such a country as this, might have been expected" (see
Catalogue, p. 11), and that it had "not as yet succeeded
in *attracting the attention,* and *obtaining the protection of*
GOVERNMENT. *(Ibid).* The Directors, although
working against wind and tide, and perpetually baffled on
the highest ground, by the adamantine wall of church exclu-

sion, have done incalculable good; but the manly avowal just quoted, proves their conviction, that they cannot, of themselves, with their own limited resources, effect their noble object; and that they have, all along, *looked to the* GOVERNMENT *of the country for its accomplishment.*

The right honourable the Select Committee of the House of Commons, on the Elgin Marbles, concluded their report with the following observations :—" Your Committee cannot dismiss this interesting subject, without submitting *to the attentive reflection of the House,* HOW HIGHLY *the cultivation of the fine arts has contributed to the* REPUTATION, CHARACTER, and DIGNITY of EVERY GOVERNMENT *by which they have been encouraged,* and how *intimately they are connected with the advancement of* EVERY THING VALUABLE IN SCIENCE, LITERATURE, and PHILOSOPHY. In contemplating the *importance and splendour to which* SO SMALL A REPUBLIC AS ATHENS *rose,* by the GENIUS and ENERGY of HER CITIZENS, *exerted in the path of such studies,* it is impossible to overlook *how transient the memory and fame of extended empires,* and *of mighty conquerors are, in comparison with those who have rendered inconsiderable states eminent, and immortalized their own names by these pursuits.* But if it be true, as we learn from history and experience, that free governments afford a soil most *suitable to the production of native talent, to the maturing of the powers of the human mind,* and *to the growth of every species of excellence,* by OPENING to MERIT THE PROSPECT of REWARD and DISTINCTION, no country can be better adapted than our own to afford an honourable asylum to these monuments of the school of *Phidias* and of the administration of *Pericles;* where, secure from

P

further injury and degradation, they may receive that admiration and homage to which they are entitled, and *serve in return as* MODELS *and* EXAMPLES *to those*, who, by knowing how to revere and appreciate them, may learn *first to imitate, and, ultimately,* TO RIVAL THEM."

Nothing can be more just or convincing than the above, coming from so high an authority as a Select Committee, and addressed to a British House of Commons, the first legislative body in the universe.. The *Elgin marbles* were purchased as a *means* for an *end.* But how can the British artists rival those of Greece and Italy, so long as the sources of public patronage, which " raised and rewarded the Grecian and Italian masters," are walled up in this country by the church exclusion of pictures, and that the Government beholds the evil without a remedy?

The right honourable Frederick Robinson, the Chancellor of the Exchequer, made the following wise observations in the House of Commons, on the 23d of Feb. 1824, when introducing the wish of Government to purchase the ANGERSTEIN collection of paintings :—" Looking *at the connection of the arts with the glory of the nation,* and *with every thing that dignifies and ennobles man in his individual capacity,* he deemed it *consistent with the principles which a great nation ought to adopt, to stand forward as* THE PATRON OF THE ARTS, and *to* GIVE LARGELY *to* THEIR SUPPORT." (*Cheers.*) " Ministers felt that *where a* LARGE COLLECTION of VALUABLE PICTURES *was offered for sale, there were many motives of liberal policy, inviting the* FORMATION OF A NATIONAL GALLERY."

These are, indeed, the liberal sentiments of an enlightened and able statesman. It is impossible to read them without feeling a sentiment of esteem and regard for the speaker.

But all these provident and invaluable purchases, the high-minded principle and public spirit of which cannot be too warmly applauded, are avowedly only a *means* " to *raise* and *reward*" *British art* and *British artists*, and to excite them to equal the artists of Greece and Italy. They are but the *weapons* to enable the British empire to win the most splendid of all her victories—the *bridge* over which she is to pass to the field of her proudest glory.—Yet, at the very time when the Chancellor of the Exchequer was acquiring such well merited-honours for himself and the ministers, in fulfilling his Majesty's gracious and paternal desire in favour of the British school, the BRITISH PUBLIC STYLE was on the point of extinction! The most promising students of history painting had made their escape from the historical field! HAYDON, who, with unshaken firmness had clung to that forlorn hope, was fast sinking, in the prime of his life and powers, into the gripe of bailiffs, and on the verge of a prison! NORTH-COTE, the painter of the death of Wat Tyler, a picture which would have obtained distinction in any age or nation, was painting for publishers, or without a commission, on the precarious prospect of chance purchasers! The Great Master, who had been for nearly half a century historical painter to the late King, the venerable founder and father of British historical painting, who had been for a long series of years looked up to as the acknowledged head of the fine arts in this country; the honoured President of the Royal Academy of painting, sculpture and architecture in England, the grand series of whose historical pictures, and the prints engraved from them, had far spread the fame of England in the arts through the world—this distinguished artist had not been dead full three years, and he too was apparently forgotten! The splendid gallery, containing an accumulated treasure of his historical pictures, the profound labours of fifty years, was, at that very hour, when the right honourable the Chancellor of the Exchequer was so eloquently and justly urging the advantages of a NATIONAL GALLERY, wholly DESERTED BY THE PUBLIC; and seemingly unthought of by the government, in the hurry and effervescence of its comprehensive plans for the national improvement and glory.

England is in a fortunate situation for adopting a great national measure, with respect to historical painting, in the noble plan of A NATIONAL GALLERY. The most august personage in the state has graciously manifested his attachment to the fine arts, and his paternal desire for their cultivation *by British artists*, as *elevated moral instruments of national improvement and glory*. The *Administration*, the *Legislature*, and the *British Institution*, have zealously concurred in this truly royal desire, and have promulgated, in different forms, the same high-minded sentiment. They have auspiciously followed up the purchase of the *Townley*, *Phygalian*, and *Elgin marbles*, by the purchase of the *Angerstein collection of paintings*, as the commencement of a NATIONAL GALLERY. In all these invaluable acquisitions for the public service, they have richly merited, and received, the thanks of their country, in spirit, though not in form. In this warm sense of gratitude we have cordially joined our very humble feelings. But a strange notion is current in certain circles, that England can acquire the glory of a genius for the highest excellence in the arts, by further purchases of fine pictures and statues from Greece, Italy, and France, without applying any of her immense means in public patronage to cultivate the grand style, and raise and reward her native artists in that department. It may be quite right to

extend our *purchases* and *importations* of fine pictures and
statues in due season; but we cannot help thinking, that
the British artists in the highest class, are objects of present consideration, as the primary means by which the
British empire can acquire true national glory in the noblest subjects of painting and sculpture, and can accom-
plish her great and praiseworthy object of vieing with the
artists of Greece and Italy.

The praise of superior intellect, the glory of genius, is
a possession beyond all price; a distinction from heaven,
which cannot be purchased by individuals or by nations,
however powerful. England possesses more fame from
the circumstance of Othello, Lear, and the other dramatic
works of our great poet, having been written by an Englishman, than she would acquire by the *purchase* of the
imperial library at Vienna, and of the royal library in the
Louvre at Paris. The possession of such a vast accession
of literary treasures on every subject, would be an immense
advantage, yet what Englishman would exchange the
honour of *being the countryman of Shakspeare* for his
share of the real or supposed honour of two such *purchased importations?* Greece derived more honour from
the *Iliad*, as the production of a Greek poet, than the
*Ptolemies* acquired by the *purchase* of the many hundred
thousand volumes in the Alexandrian library. Did the
bookseller who paid ten pounds for the manuscript of Milton's Paradise Lost, acquire the glory of that sublime
poem by his purchase? Surely not. Can England sell
or alienate the national glory which she derives from the
compositions of Shakspeare and Milton? No; certainly.
Can France barter away or transfer the national glory
which she derives from the dramatic works of *Racine* or
*Corneille?* Again we reply in the negative. The purchase

by France or England, of all the divine works of Raphael
and Michael Angelo (if they were portable), in the Vatican, would not acquire the national glory of those works
for the *purchasers;* because the glory of having produced
them belongs to Italy: and that glory is her national property, which she can neither sell nor alienate, nor be de-
prived of by any human power.

In 1810, France, with all the finest productions of the
pencil and chisel in the Louvre, collected from Italy, Spain,
Germany, and Flanders, was in reality no more than *the
keeper* of a splendid spectacle for the world to gaze at.
Her military pride was flattered by her having won them
with the sword, but their excellence as works of art was no
addition to the just reputation of the French School. She
appeared before other nations like the daw in borrowed
feathers. A nation must either use such foreign acquisitions as a means to rival the great masters of the renowned
ages, or she must appear like a negro flashing a torch-light
in his own face to expose his darkness and deformity. A
modern state can rest her hope of rivaling the ancients
only on the one ground of applying a portion of her *public
patronage* to the support of her native artists in the cultivation of the *public style*: by that mode alone she can
convert her *purchased* master-pieces of the old schools
into a means of national glory to herself. France wisely
endeavoured to do so, and *has done so;* but all Frenchmen
felt that she derived more national fame from having produced the Seven Sacraments, painted by a Frenchman,
her profound master, Nicolas Poussin, than she acquired by
the possession of all the vast collection from other countries in the Louvre. Italy retained the imperishable glory
of her fine paintings and sculpture after she had lost them.
France acquired no share in the glory of having produced

those master-pieces, although she had obtained possession
of them. Whether fine works of art are acquired by
France, by England, or by any other country, by *gold*, by
*steel*, or by gift, by purchase, by force, or by courtesy, the
glory that belongs to the genius that produced them is *national*; it is a growth rooted in the soil, the indefeasible inheritance of a people, and not to be transferred to any other
clime or country.

It is clear that England derives more glory from having
produced the *Marriage à-la-Mode*,* by Hogarth, than by
having purchased and imported the Cartoons of Raphael:
the former, as a native British growth, is an indestructible
national honour: the latter, as the production of an Italian
master, is an eternal honour to the genius of Italy. A fire
might deprive England of the possession, the benefit, and
the just pride of those inestimable compositions by Raphael:
but neither fire, the sword, nor any possible accident of
time or chance can deprive England of the fame of Hogarth's genius: even if all his works were destroyed, their
fame, like that of the Grecian painters, whose pictures have
perished so many ages ago, would live for ever in contemporary records. SIR JOHN FLEMING LEICES-
TER, in giving Hilton a commission to paint the *Europa;*
Lord Mulgrave, in giving Haydon a commission to paint
Dentatus; Sir George Beaumont, by giving the same artist
a commission to paint Macbeth; and the late Marquis of
Exeter, in employing STOTHARD to display his elegant

---

* We beg our readers not to misunderstand us here: we, by no means,
place in one class, compositions so different as Hogarth's *Marriage à-la-
Mode*, and the Cartoons of Raphael; nor do we advert to them as works
which admit of comparison. But we have no hesitation in avowing our
admiration of Hogarth's powers as a genius of the highest order in his
own department, upon the level of familiar life and manners.

imagination in embellishing Burghley; did more for the honour of England than if they had discovered and *imported* the celebrated Cartoon of Pisa by Michael Angelo, which the Italian writers suppose to have been destroyed by the envy of *Baccio Bandinelli.* Christ Healing the Sick, Christ Rejected, and Death on the Pale Horse, the three last grand compositions by WEST, confer more glory on the British name, than could accrue to England from any purchase or importation of sculpture or paintings from Greece or Italy. The late King, by commissioning WEST to paint English history in Windsor Castle, and the sublime series of compositions from the Revelations, for the intended chapel-royal, contributed more to the glory of the British name and the advancement of the fine arts, than if his Majesty by the help of Aladdin's Genii, had *imported* the *Vatican* entire, with all its wonders of Italian genius, and set it up in Pall-Mall as a national gallery.

After the establishment of some constant source of public patronage for elevated British works of art, it may be most unwise to lose any fair opportunity of acquiring first class specimens of painting and sculpture from Italy or Greece, chosen with the same good taste, liberality, and public spirit, as have been evinced in selecting the collections already purchased by the Government. But it is a point of wisdom and absolute necessity to let the appropriation of a fund by Government for the patronage of British excellence in the public style, keep pace with those munificent and praiseworthy purchases of ancient master-pieces. If a sum of one hundred thousand pounds were voted to-morrow by the wisdom of Parliament for the advancement of the fine arts as instruments of moral improvement and national distinction, it might be wise to expend £50,000. of that sum for fresh acquisitions of *first-rate spe-*

cimens of the old schools for the national gallery, AFTER
having devoted the other £50,000. to the remuneration of
British artists in that high style, by which alone, this country can hope, in the sound opinion of the British Institution,
to command the homage of foreign nations. What we
mean is, that after £140,000. have been so wisely expended
on ancient works of art as a *means*, one half of every hundred pounds expended in future on the fine arts, would
be well employed on THE END, that is, in carrying into
effect the noble object of vieing with the Grecian and Italian
masters, as proposed by the Select Committee on the Elgin
Marbles, and by the Directors of the patriotic association
just mentioned. The cause of just apprehension at present,
arises solely from what has NOT *yet* BEEN DONE, or
rather from *what remains to be done*, and because that
*nothing has yet been done* to *counteract the great national
obstacle, church exclusion*, and appropriate any portion of our
immense revenue in *patronage* of the *public style*. This
apprehension does not by any means lessen our unqualified
applause of every purchase of statues and pictures hitherto
made by Government. The pride of possessing the treasures of Grecian and Roman art, is not only just, but highly
laudable, when not indulged, as it has been in other countries, from a fallacious notion that the possession of such
foreign treasures is, in itself, a proof of a national taste and
genius for the fine arts, and a source of national glory to
the possessors. The danger of such a mistake, when cou-
pled with the anti-historical spirit of the age, created by
the great national obstacle, the church exclusion of pictures,
must impede, and perhaps defeat, any plan of Government
to patronize the public style, with a view to vie with the
ancients, and render British genius worthy the homage of
foreign nations.

Q

It is clear that it is by British genius, by productions of the British pencil and chisel alone, that this country can hope to employ the fine arts as instruments for raising and extending the British character in foreign countries. Until the State appropriates a fund for the patronage of the public style, we can no more hope to raise national character, or acquire the reputation of excellence in the fine arts by importing fine pictures and statues, and placing them in a NATIONAL GALLERY, than a Manchester manufacturer can hope to reap a profit from storing ship-loads of raw cotton in his warehouses under lock and key for years. It is not by possessing the articles in a useless or an unused state that the end for which they were purchased can be obtained. The ancient pictures and statues, if viewed in their proper light, are as much a *raw material* for setting British hands and British heads to work, as the unspun cotton. But the difference is this; the Lancashire manufacturer has a sure market and plenty of customers for his cottons when they are manufactured, and the British artists, who are called on to vie with the great Italian and Grecian masters, have neither a commission nor a buyer in that high department which forms the field of competition. The conclusion is just as it might be expected: the Manchester man finds plenty of hands, and he carries the day against the world, while the great Grecian and Italian masters are, at present, left without a competitor, in quiet possession of the Homeric field. The great *national obstacle* mocks at the public spirited efforts of the King, Lords, and Commons, so far as they have gone: it mocks at the persevering patriotism of the British Institution: it plunges them up to the throat in an *impossibility* like that of *Glendower*. They may call British students and artists

to vie with the ancients, but the gibing reply of the *foul
fiend* is upon them, with a vengeance ;—

"*Aye! but will they come?*"

Who obeyed their call with more high-minded alacrity
than Haydon and his pupils? Well, and where are they?
And what was his reward? Oh shame! England! when will
you be true to your own genius in the arts? When the
goal of glory is the KING'S BENCH, who would not be
an historical painter!

There will be some prospect of competing with the ancients when the Government is authorised to address this
encouragement to the artists who have evinced powers in
the historical department.—There are the master-piéces of
Greece and Italy, which the state has purchased at the
paternal suggestion of his Majesty, and by the wisdom and
liberality of Parliament: they are placed before you, not to
abash you by comparison, but to rouse your emulation; a
public fund is lodged in the treasury " to *raise* and *reward*"
British merit;—here are the commissions which you are to
execute for the embellishment of the specified public buildings:—Go and obtain " *the homage of foreign nations*"
for your country, by exerting your genius for her glory.

If ever a nation acquires national glory by the purchase
of works of art, it is when she nobly applies her means and
her public patronage to purchase the chief works in the
highest class of excellence by her native artists. There is,
at present, not a British historical picture in the British
National Gallery. But the unrivalled series of the Marriage à-la-Mode, with his own Portrait, by *Hogarth*; the
admirable Village Festival, by *Wilkie*; and the magnificent
Portrait of Lord Heathfield, by *Reynolds*; on account of
their standard excellence in their class, and their being the
works of British artists, are entitled to peculiar notice,

We have offered these observations, because there are some grave persons who draw their chief arguments from their bankers' books, and conceive that genius and glory are purchaseable in foreign countries, and can be imported like rum, sugar, tobacco, and cotton, or any other saleable commodity. Such persons imagine, that in buying the *Townley, Phygalian, and Elgin* Marbles, and the *Anger-stein* collection of paintings, the Government has established the national character of England for national taste and genius in the highest style of sculpture and painting. These confident reasoners speak as if the probable extinction of the public style in this country was a mere nothing, and that it was as easy to make up A NATIONAL GALLERY full of *imported glory*, as it is to stock a warehouse in Thames-street with West India produce. We confess, however, that we are a little dull upon this delicate point. We have endeavoured to show that genius, and the glory of high excellence in the arts, are a *native growth* which cannot be transplanted: they have " *a local habitation,*" from which all the armies in the universe cannot drive them; and " *a name,*" of which all the gold in the mines of South America cannot obtain possession.

We trust we have replied in the preceding remarks, to the objections of those who have so unthinkingly blamed the Government for the admission of a few fine English pictures into the national gallery in Pall-mall. We confess that we consider the purchase to have been a measure of wisdom and national feeling; because British glory in the fine arts, like British glory in arms, must be the offspring of British mind and of British genius, worked up by British hands, by British pencils, and British chisels. It must be of native growth, fostered by public patronage, and reaped by public spirit from our own intellectual soil. If we were to *purchase* all the fine pictures and statues on the Continent for a national gallery, we should be, after all, no more than the keeper of a treasure, while foreign nations would possess the glory of having produced it. A national gallery in England, to answer its *end* and *title*, ought not only to comprehend fine examples of the old schools for study, but also to be rich in national, that is, in *British* pictures. We have showed that the British Institution, to whose exertions and enlarged views the arts and the country are so much indebted, publicly announced in 1811, the important fact that they had purchased Mr. West's Christ Healing the Sick, *for the purpose of making it the* foundation stone of A BRITISH GALLERY: and undoubtedly that distinguished body in doing so, acted from their conviction that a British gallery was absolutely necessary as *one of the means* towards enabling the British artists to vie with the masters of Greece and Italy. The splendid collection of pictures by the late PRESIDENT WEST, now exhibiting in the spacious rooms erected by his sons, offers a golden opportunity to Government of proceeding with their excellent purpose of forming a national gallery of fine pictures from the foreign old schools and from the British masters.

We mention the purchase of Mr. West's splendid series of historical pictures on public grounds; that is, *first*, on the ground of their high, indisputable, and acknowledged merits, and their being the productions of a great British master. We humbly conceive that the proposed purchase of them would prove a benefit to British students, an encouragement to all British artists, and would confer a national mark of distinction on the British school. We sincerely think that such a purchase would be a national acquisition equally honourable to the memory of the great founder and father of the British school, and to the true

British feeling, good taste, and enlarged views of the Government. The merits of West stand proudly forward, not only in the testimony of his works, but in the unbiassed testimony of his professional contemporaries, and of his country. We show our indifference to the charge of repetition, when we here recapitulate the following unbiassed opinions of a writer of sound taste and elegant fancy, a gentleman critically skilled in the works of the ancient and modern schools—" Christ Healing the Sick assumes SO HIGH A RANK in *graphic composition, as to fear no future decline from its present just estimation.* The GREAT MASTER OF COMPOSITION from whose hand it came, *holds a place in this respect* AMONGST WHATEVER MODERN or ANCIENT SCHOOLS *have produced* OF EMINENCE. Above the *sportive,* desultory trains of *Venetian grouping, he ranks with the* MORE CHASTE COMPOSERS *of the* FLORENTINE and LOMBARD SCHOOLS, and *surpassing many, is excelled by few.* The merits of the picture exhibited at the British Gallery are not new in the artist. *Nearly fifty years of his life have been passed in the production of works of similar worth.*"—(Prince Hoare's Epochs of the Arts, p. 221.)

Mr. Prince Hoare, in the same work, terms the late President, " the great historical painter of our day." The late SIR HENRY RAEBURN, whose powers as a painter, and judgment in works of art were so highly and justly appreciated by his country, in a letter now before us, mentions Mr. West thus:—" The great British historical painter of the age, whose works would rank him in the best ages of art in Italy among the great masters."— Mr. SHEE, in the extract which we have inserted in a former page, from his " *Commemoration of Reynolds,*" rejoiced in the public patronage conferred by the British Institution on " this GREAT and VENERABLE ARTIST, who STANDS AT THE HEAD, *not only* OF THE ARTS IN THIS COUNTRY, but WHO HAS PRODUCED WORKS WHICH TAKE THE LEAD OF HIS COMPETITORS IN EVERY OTHER COUNTRY IN EUROPE."

We have already showed, that the *British Institution,* with honest exultation, in the true spirit of national pride and of public patronage, expressed a hope to England, that " THE COUNTRY of REYNOLDS and WEST" would not merely *imitate,* but would *rival* the *Grecian and Italian* masters. We refer to that fact again, to place it in a new light. That body, consisting of the first amateur judges, in whatever relates to the fine arts, thus united these two great British masters with the glory of the British empire by the imperishable links of honour. They held them up to Europe as the two EYES of the British School, the two great luminaries of the arts in the modern world. We have also, in a former page, stated, that the public exposition of principles in which this just homage was paid to British genius, was issued under the sanction of their late Majesties, of his Royal Highness the Prince of Wales, of sixteen additional members of the royal family, of thirty-nine British peers, and of a list of gentry of distinguished taste, talents, and public spirit. The document, so honourable to the illustrious, noble, and eminent names which are prefaced to it, is a matter of national record. Nor was this an empty compliment; it was followed up by the signal proof of their sincerity, in their purchase of a single picture by the pencil of WEST, at the unparalleled remuneration of three thousand guineas! Here is a pledge to support the interests of historical painting in the memory of West, as an honour to the country, which is a tower of strength at the present moment! A testimony to his fame which can never be obliterated or forgotten.

After having recapitulated the high estimate of Prince Hoare, of Sir Henry Raeburn, of Mr. Shee, and of the British Institution, we shall recapitulate some points from the discourse of SIR THOMAS LAWRENCE, which we have inserted in a former page. Sir Thomas places the names of REYNOLDS and WEST, the two great luminaries of the arts in the modern world, together, with the lamenting expression of a noble mind, that the powers of the latter "DESERVED NOT THE CONTRAST OF THEIR PRESENT FORTUNE." We most sincerely partake in this painful conviction, and we deplore the melancholy fact, that the pictorial hill of fame is of a richer soil near its base, that it becomes less productive in its ascent, and that

> " Shadows, clouds, and darkness rest upon
> Its barren head."

But we trust, that the members of the Government will be true to their own character and to the interests of the British School, by extending the public patronage of the State to the works of the great British historical painter after his decease, on the broad grounds of public policy, justice, and honourable feeling.

In this recapitulation we remind our readers, that the present President described the grand series of Mr. West's earlier compositions from sacred and profane history, as "not only superior to any former productions of English art, but far surpassing contemporary merit on the continent, and un-

*equalled* at any period below the school of the Caracci;" that is, unequalled by any of the Italian masters for the last two hundred years. We have, also, already noticed, that Sir Thomas Lawrence afterwards mentioned the grand picture of Christ Healing the Sick in the Temple, as *a greater display of power;* and then noticed his still later productions, (*Christ Rejected,* and *Death on the Pale Horse,*) as works of "*more arduous subjects,* of *greater magnitude,* and, IF POSSIBLE, *more powerfully impressive.*" The " *if possible,*" strikingly attests the power of the former pictures, and the "*astonishing abilities*" of the two stupendous works which crowned the close of his long, honoured, and laborious life! The ascending scale of this great master's excellence is distinctly marked by his former pupil, up to his eightieth year, in which he finished the last of these sublime compositions. Persons of ordinary minds generally exhibit a decay of their bodily and mental faculties together; but men of superior genius retain their intellectual powers after the decay of their bodily strength. *Michael Angelo* was fast approaching his seventieth year when he finished his prodigious work, the *Last Judgment,* in the *Sistine Chapel.*

It is known that Sir Thomas Lawrence, when lately upon the continent, visited Rome, and the principal cities of Italy, and that he gratified his fine taste and professional desire of improvement, by inspecting the chief works of the old masters. We here *recapitulate* a remarkable fact already adverted to. The present President, in his address to the students in the Royal Academy, stated, that when enjoying this feast abroad, he found, on comparing the grand compositions of West in his memory, with the master-pieces of Italy which he was examining, the works of

R

the great British historical painter *rose in his estimation by the comparison.*

The third President, impressed with a strong sense of WEST'S genius and profound science, and of the importance of his works as materials of study in the formation of a British School, addressed the following advice to the Students; an advice to drink deeply of the learning in those fine compositions. The sentence is short, but it contains volumes for the consideration of Government in their purchase of pictures for the *British National Gallery.* "But, *though unnoticed by the public,* THE GALLERY of Mr. West REMAINS, GENTLEMEN, FOR YOU, and EXISTS FOR YOUR INSTRUCTION."—Here is the most important directing truth laid down by the very highest professional authority, and coming from a mind of unclouded talent and unbiassed integrity. What sounder counsel can the Government have for its guidance? What a proud triumph is this for England! The students of painting in the Royal Academy are sent by the present President, not to Rome, nor to Florence, to Venice, to Bologna, Parma, nor to Paris, for improvement; but, in the first instance to the historical gallery of West, the founder and father of the British historical school of painting, and, for a long series of years, the acknowledged head of the arts in the British empire. May the words of Sir Thomas Lawrence, through the wisdom of Government, prove prophetic! May the series of West's historical pictures *exist* and *remain* for ever *unseparated,* for the instruction of the British students, and the glory of the British School!

We insert the following extracts from a critique on Mr. West's Death on the Pale Horse, in 1817, in a quarterly work, some years discontinued, and remarkable for its subsequent attempts to lower the professional character of that great master. "Till very lately, NO ONE ARTIST SUSTAINED THE DIGNITY OF EPIC and HISTORIC ART but the VENERABLE PAINTER *of* THE PRESENT PICTURE, who, *for nearly* THREE-FOURTHS OF A CENTURY, *stood almost alone* as AN HISTORICAL PAINTER; and *during the whole of which time he has held* A REPUTATION DESERVEDLY BRILLIANT. *Patronized* by HIS SOVEREIGN, his best works decorate the royal halls of Windsor; yet *no individual or private patronage encouraged* HIS SOLITARY EFFORTS *to maintain the rank of an historical painter."* "The pictorial patriarch received abundantly the rewards of his steadiness, his *perseverance,* and *chivalrous adoration* of his *art.* Placed BY HIS TALENTS AT THE HEAD of THE ENGLISH SCHOOL, &c. &c." The above testimony of Mr. West's genius, and of his solitary and enthusiastic devotion to historical painting, is contained in an unfavourable review of his picture. And the same publication some time before contained the following just tribute of applause:—" No one can so well spare praise as OUR *at present* GREATEST HISTORICAL PAINT-ER; we will therefore borrow of HIS RICHES, to bestow on those who are *less richly endowed,* or *less bold in bending the great* historic bow."—When such were the confessions of Mr. *West's* assailants, we may fairly stand acquitted of partiality in our very humble testimony to his merits.

In addition to these written and published evidences of the science, the power, and grandeur displayed in Mr. West's works, we proceed proudly in our recapitulation to the triumphant record of facts—the twenty-seven annual elections of the great British historical painter of our day, to fill the high and dignified public office of President of the Royal Academy of painting, sculpture, and architecture in England. This may be very fairly termed a national *elevation* indeed! Would the Royal Academicians, with all their jealous sense of professional reputation, their conflicting pride, their honourable ambition of precedence, their eager competition as men of genius, and their feelings of self-respect as gentlemen, have unanimously and voluntarily, *twenty-seven times*, elected any but an artist of the highest claims to stand, as Mr. Shee has termed it, at their head, and at the head of the arts in the British empire? The question needs no answer. It is to be remembered, that a year for deliberation intervened between each of these elections: and that each was a public act, recorded in the presence of the world: that they extended over a period of at least twenty-seven years, and that each was honoured with the royal signature and sanction. Here is the highest possible professional testimony to the powers of Mr. West as an historical painter, and to the high excellence in drawing, character, expression, composition, and colouring, exhibited in the grand series of pictures which he has left behind him; and which now offer such noble materials to the Government for enriching the national gallery of England with acknowledged masterpieces of the British pencil.

Besides these twenty-seven annual elections by the Royal Academicians of England, we have to *recapitulate*, that the sight of his pictures by foreign artists and amateurs on their travels in England, and the fame of his genius spread abroad by the fine series of prints from his historical compositions, induced the artists of the different academies of painting, sculpture, and architecture on the continent, unanimously to elect him a member of their several institutions. In the United States of America he was also

unanimously elected a member of the academy of painting
at New York, and likewise of the academy of painting at
Philadelphia. We repeat it, that in every country where
the fine arts are honoured and incorporated in a NATIONAL
FORM, the enrolment of WEST'S name has been deemed
an addition of honour to their body by its members.

HAYLEY'S verses on West's style, are so just, as far as
they extend, that we insert them here, as the *criticism* of
a poet of elegant fancy, who had inspected the best pictures on the continent, with much warm feeling and discri-
mination of their beauties. His love of the fine arts, and
his zeal for the advancement of the British School, are
strikingly evinced in his Epistles on Painting, from which
we borrow the following extract:—

" Supremely skill'd, the varied group to place,
And range the crowded scene with easy grace;
To finish parts, yet not impair the whole,
But on the impassion'd action fix the soul;
Through wand'ring throngs the patriot chief to guide,
The shame of CARTHAGE, as of ROME the pride;
Or while the bleeding victor yields his breath,
Give the bright lesson of heroic death:
Such are thy merits, WEST, by Virtue's hand,
BUILT ON THE HUMAN HEART THY PRAISE
SHALL STAND,
While dear to glory, in her guardian fane,
The names of REGULUS and WOLFE remain."
(Epistles on Painting, Ep. II. l. 177, &c.)

This poet was much struck by West's Death of Bayard,
and he endeavoured to rouse Romney to paint the death of
Sir Philip Sydney, in emulation of its merits. Romney
possessed a strong desire to paint history, but he prudently
forbore from an attempt to vie with the great historical

painter of the age.  Even the publication of the following verses failed of their intended effect:—

> " Shall BAYARD, glorious in his dying hour,
> Of GALLIC CHIVALRY the fairest flow'r,—
> Shall his pure blood in *British colours* flow,
> And Britain, on her canvass, fail to show
> Her wounded SIDNEY, Bayard's perfect peer,
> Sidney, her knight, without reproach or fear,
> O'er whose pale corse heroic worth should bend,
> And mild humanity embalm her friend?
> Oh! Romney, in his hour of death we find
> *A subject worthy of thy feeling mind*," &c.
>
> <div align="right">(<i>Ibid</i>, l. 436, &c.)</div>

It required some courage to stand out this sort of public friendly challenge.  But ROMNEY had yielded to the anti-historical spirit of the time; was then making between 3 and £4,000. a year by painting portraits, and looked up to West with too just a sense of his powers to venture upon the encounter.  POPE, with all his fine imagination and exquisite sense of beauty as a poet, from not having had his *eyes educated* by opportunities of viewing good pictures early in life, was but a very indifferent judge of painting.  He mistook the tame, vapid portraits of his friend and drawing master, JERVAS, for the productions of a second Titian, and, in his epistle to that fortunate manu-facturer of stained canvas, flattered him that the beauties of his day, should

> " Bloom in his colours for a thousand years."

HAYLEY had studied pictures, and was by far the best critic on the subject among the British poets.

The candour and impartiality of SIR THOMAS LAW-RENCE are proverbial: his frankness and public spirit are well known; his love of his profession, his distinguished

genius, and the number of his brilliant works, confer
an important weight on his high opinion of Mr. West's
historical pictures. His matured taste and judgment must
be conclusive in any estimate of excellence in works of art.
The relative circumstances of the occasion, and the spontaneous manner in which he pointed out WEST'S gallery
as a SCHOOL of INSTRUCTION for the students of the
Royal Academy, must, in every reflecting mind, convert his
professional advice to them into a proof of *West's* invaluable
science and powers, " strong as holy writ." An uncalled-
for opinion thus given by so eminent an artist, in his character of President of the Royal Academy, as a lesson of
direction *to the Students,* is so free from every thing like
an influence, that it is impossible to doubt its origin in an
entire conviction. What a guiding light for the Government and Parliament to act upon? What a fortunate opportunity to hearten up the young artists, and maintain the
character of the British School, by purchasing those productions of British genius, to place them in the national
gallery as lessons for future British students, and specimens of British history painting for the contemplation of
foreigners. The liberality with which Sir Thomas Lawrence
recently purchased THE PANDORA, by that *inspired*
LYRIC PAINTER, ETTY,* is an evidence of his desire

---

* The elegance of ideal forms, and the picturesque graces of the most
felicitous grouping are combined in the works of this admirable artist,
with a colouring as rich in oppositions, as fresh, as vivid, and delicious, as
that of Titian or Paolo Veronese, but in general with something more of
the glittering silvery tones of the latter. His carnations are flesh itself.
The living originality, the breathing, burning spirit of his tints have not
been surpassed by any artist (whose works we have seen) since the days of
Giorgione himself. If ever painting merited the character of " *mute
poetry,*" the charming productions of this bewitching artist's imagination
are entitled to that distinction. As our opinion of his merits has been

to bring forward *British genius*, and to reward the merit of the living with the same manly promptitude, which he has manifested in doing justice to the merits of the dead. The mild dignity with which he sustained the rank of President of the Royal Academy of England, at Paris, Vienna, Rome, and the other courts which he lately visited on the continent, on a mission from his Majesty, and the signal display of power with which he executed his royal patron's commissions, are still spoken of by foreigners and the British nobility and gentry, who were then abroad, in terms of esteem and admiration. Less powerful and less studied in his *chiaro-oscuro*, less rich in contrast and splendour of colouring, his best works are equal in harmony to those of *Sir Joshua Reynolds*, more simple, more sweet, and true in the flesh tints. Far superior to that great master in drawing, he is equal to him in the taste of his dispositions and attitudes, in the choice of his accessories, and in the lively expression of his likenesses. His male portraits have the courtly and easy air of well-bred gentlemen, and no painter but *Vandyke* and *Reynolds* ever painted a lovely female of rank with so much enchanting grace, and so happy a union of fashionable refinement and natural elegance.

If ever the works of any painter belonged to his country, the works of West are peculiarly entitled to that distinction, on account of their merits, of the services which he has rendered to the British School, and the honour which his performances have obtained for the empire. He was the first British historical painter whose genius raised and ennobled art by the power of his hand as a draftsman, by the

for some years upon public record, we shall not here add any further remarks on the *Pandora*, which we have, day after day, examined with unabated delight.

elevated choice of his subject, the grandeur of its treatment, and the impressive moral which it conveyed.   There
was then little or no knowledge of the arts in this country.
Painting, as in Holland, was obliged to depend on individual patronage, and to follow the caprice of the crowd.
Reynolds, when sixty-seven years old, after he had left off
painting, frankly owned this fact just before his death :—
" I have taken another course, one more suited to my abilities, and *to the* TASTE *of the* TIMES *in which I live.*"
—Opie (in the Biographical Dictionary of the Painters)
has blamed that great master, we think rather inconsider-
ately, for this compliance with the times.   But no other
artist, even with his peculiarly fine powers, could have done
more, or perhaps so much, as Reynolds.   He did wonders
under the heaviest disadvantages.   The state of the public
mind may be guessed at from the description of a contemporary artist :—" NOTHING COULD EXCEED
THE IGNORANCE OF A PEOPLE who were themselves
learned, ingenious, and highly cultivated in all things *but*
*the arts of design.*"—(Mem. of Sir J. R. by Joseph Farrington, R.A.)   We are not to be surprised, therefore,
that West's PYLADES AND ORESTES, in 1766, became,
as Northcote has stated it, " A MATTER OF MUCH
SURPRISE ;" or that, in 1768, when his Agrippina
landing with the ashes of Germanicus, was exhibited, the
chief practice of painting lay on the level of fashionable life.   For the very few rare deviations from the
direct course of unmixed portrait, the country was indebted
to the charming fancy and honourable endeavours of Reynolds.   The dignified aims of the historical pencil, as an
intellectual instrument, correct drawing and costume, deep
sentiment, and purity of design, were an unknown language,
slighted and contemned.   We have showed in a former

S

page, that the powers of *Hogarth*, as a *painter*, the grandeur of *Wilson*, and the admirable rural scenery, cattle,
and rustic English figures by *Gainsborough*, the grave historical nobleness and simple dignity of *West's* invention,
were misunderstood and despised. The popular branch of
painting engrossed the attention of the literature, the press,
and of the fashionable world; and the anti-historical spirit,
bred by the great national obstacle, would hardly permit a
word of praise to any picture but a portrait. Painting
was merely considered a seductive show, or as the gilding
of a decorated apartment. Even among the better informed amateurs, the witcheries of colour, and of light and sha-
dow, splendid harmony, and richness of effect, freedom of
penciling, delicacies of touch, and a tasteful disposition,
depending chiefly upon linear elegance, were prized as the
chief merits of the art. The most extravagant praises and
the highest honours were lavished upon technical merits
which lay upon the SURFACE; were chiefly calculated to
appeal to the eye, and might be termed the *art-magic* of
the *hand*. We are warranted by the picture, by public
documents, dates, and indisputable facts, in stating, as an
act of justice, that no such picture as the *Agrippina*, in
elevation of subject, dignified treatment, purity of design,
drawing, and costume, had ever before been executed by a
British artist. The *Agrippina* was not only, in these re-
spects, above all contemporary art, but we have Sir Thomas Lawrence's estimate, that it was unequalled by any
of the painters upon the continent since the school of the
CARACCI, that is, for two hundred years. We, as confidently affirm, that no such elevated historical subject was
painted by any British artist for some years afterwards,
except by *West:* and during the ensuing fifty years, West
continued to produce pictures of equal worth. (Hoare's

Epochs of Art.)  The artist who had the manliness, during so long a life, to make almost a solitary stand against the old *national evil*, the church exclusion of pictures, and against the bad taste of the time, must have possessed enthusiastic attachment to his art, great firmness of mind, high moral dignity, and disinterestedness.  The British painter who, by the generous devotion of his pencil to the noblest aim of his profession first brought British painting into direct association with the THRONE, and raised it into an object of national honour and importance in the mind of his SOVEREIGN, rendered the British school a service of incalculable importance.  For this service the British artists and their country are indebted to WEST, and this is the crisis when they are bound to manifest their gratitude.

The chief share which Mr. West had in inducing his late Majesty to found the Royal Academy, and to take the British School under his special protection and gracious patronage, forms another claim upon the gratitude of his professional brethren and of the public.  His aversion to intrigue, and his straight-forward sincerity, were evinced by his having so disinterestedly canvassed for the election of Reynolds, although the dignity of President, lay, as it were, within his own reach, from his powers as the first eminent historical painter of the age, from the personal favour in which he stood with the King, and from the known indisposition of the artists to elect Reynolds.  The painters having elected *Lambert, Hayman,* and *Kirby,* from 1760 to 1768, and the difference between them and Reynolds, leave no doubt that if West had been of an ambitious turn, and had availed himself of his just claims, as the painter of Agrippina and his other historical pictures, or had made use of his interest with the Archbishop of York, and the King, he might have procured his own election with less trouble,

and infinitely with more justice, than either Lambert, Hayman, or Kirby.  Their elections passed without noise or
opposition : *why* should not his ?   To this rare instance of
self-denial in this mild and amiable man, his great contemporary, Reynolds, was indebted for his election to the rank
of President, which produced his knighthood ; and  the
world is indebted to the same primary cause for the golden
Discourses of Reynolds.   Barry, in his letter to the Dile-
tanti Society, has intimated his opinion, that his rank as
President was a chief cause of Reynolds's few noble exertions in history late in life.   We will not determine this
point ; but the fact is certain, that Reynolds's first historic
attempt, THE UGOLINO, was not finished nor exhibited
until 1773, when he was in the fiftieth year of his age,
and nearly five years after he had been elected President
of the Royal Academy.   On a view of the several circumstances last mentioned, it becomes a question, whether any
other British artist has been more influential in advancing the
interests of the British School, and raising it into dignified
estimation, than WEST.   The main spring of all was the
*Agrippina.*
     In addition to these meritorious claims, his having sus-
tained the character of historical painting during half a
century, in which he was almost a solitary instance of ad-
herence to that unpopular department, is another title to
esteem and regard.   There can be no doubt but that he
could have made much more than his allowance of £1000.
a year from the King's privy purse, if he had complied
with the taste of the times, and painted portraits.   There
are twenty portrait painters in London now, for one portrait painter then in the metropolis, and whoever started
with talents, was sure of a fashionable run of business, as it
has been termed.   *Romney,* and even *Liotard,* each in their

turn, divided the patronage of the town with Reynolds. Romney had a craving wish to obtain distinction as a painter of history, but the great national obstacle, the *church exclu-. sion* of pictures, stared him in the face, and intimidated him from the attempt. FUSELI, his eloquent biographer, thus bears testimony to his passion for fame, and the appalling spirit which turned him from his purpose.—" His residence at Rome was distinguished by assiduous and solitary study, and at his return he seemed inclined TO DEVOTE HIMSELF ENTIRELY TO HISTORIC PAINTING; but the *opinions of his friends, his own fears*, and the *taste of the public*, soon determined him to abandon that pursuit, and the unprofitable visions of Michelangiolo and Shakspeare, soon gave way to the more substantial allurements of portrait ; his rooms were now thronged with nobles, esquires, ministers, the *elegantes*, the belles, and literati of the day, and he *divided the tribute of fashion with Reynolds and Gainsborough.*" In this pursuit, for a considerable period, he cleared from 3 to £4000. a year, and retired in 1799, in his 64th year, " weak and *opulent*," to Kendal.  From our impartial view of the circumstances and taste of the times, and of West's facility in catching a likeness, and painting a portrait, we have no doubt that if he had listened to *fears*, and the *advice of his friends*, like *Romney,* he would have had his rooms thronged with fashionable sitters, and would have realised a noble independent fortune long before he had reached his 82d year.  If we average his probable income by portraits even so low as £2000. a year, he must have sacrificed fifty or sixty thousand pounds in his fifty-six years practice, from 1764 to 1820, by his heroic and constant attachment to historical painting.  As the cultivation of historical painting is now acknowledged, and has been formally declared by the

Government, the Parliament, and the British Institution, to be an object of essential importance to the national improvement and glory, we may, on fair and undeniable grounds affirm, that the painter, who for fifty-six years kept alive the sacred flame of that sublime art in this country, and sacrificed a noble income by so doing, can never, with any consistency or honourable feeling, be remembered or spoken of but as a GREAT PUBLIC BENEFACTOR.

From 1746 to 1773, Reynolds, with an honourable ambition of professional fame, and a public-spirited desire of raising his art in the estimation of his country, was anxious to paint history; but, from the benighted state of the public mind, owing to the confirmed effect of the great national obstacle, he deemed it more prudent and profitable to comply with the *taste of the times*, and to paint the article in daily demand. He considered himself to be walled out of the historical field. In 1816, SIR THOMAS LAWRENCE, before the Committee on the Elgin Marbles, with great nobleness and candour owned, that he also wished to paint history, but that he had seldom done so. Here again, the appalling national obstacle, crying, as it were, aloud, no commission! no purchaser! no market! repressed the exertions of genius, and

> " Froze the genial current of the soul."

Where church exclusion has thus, in the mind's eye, written in black and dismal letters over the door of every student of history painting,

> "*The Road to Ruin,*"

we are not to be surprised that so many men of high spirit and great genius have been deterred from the practice, by the dread of public neglect, poverty, disgrace, and a prison; but we may hope, in the wisdom of Government, that

some effectual remedy will be soon provided by the State to
counteract the great national evil. Surely an immediate
remedy will be applied, when we see, that from the day
of poor *John Bossam*, in the reign of Edward VI., to
the present hour, the national obstacle has operated as a
general preventative to the exertions of British genius, and
where, among those who have been prevented, we number the
first and third Presidents of the Royal Academy of England,
two artists so highly gifted by nature, so distinguished for
practical powers, and so alike in those admirable qualities
which have deservedly won the esteem and affection of the
highest circles in society. Surely, while we pay the full
tribute of applause to the excellence of these two eminent
painters, we may be allowed to observe, that the unosten-
tatious resolute stand which WEST made, during fifty-six
years, against the great national evil of the arts, and the
courageous example which he set to others by so doing, are
worthy of record and due praise. What true friend of the
British School can refuse his commendation of the persevering enthusiasm with which, during that long period, the
late President maintained the dignity of that style, by which
*alone* (it is now generally acknowledged) this country can
ever hope to employ the arts as a moral instrument to elevate the national character, and to obtain the homage of
foreign nations.

Besides the claims which West's paintings have to a
place in the *British national gallery*, from their approved
merits, from their being productions of British genius, and
from the invaluable services which he rendered to the
British School, we conceive that the purchase would
contribute to remove a very prevalent opinion, that to
study history painting is to adopt a profession which must
involve the individual for life in public neglect, difficulty,

and distress ; and expose his family to be left without any certain provision at his decease. The names of *Barry* and of *Haydon,* and the desertion of West's gallery, are at present sufficient to terrify the most enthusiastic mind from attempting history painting. Sir Joshua Reynolds has delivered his opinion, that the discouragements arising from the great national obstacle, the church exclusion of pictures, must have the effect of preventing the study of historical painting in this country. "To those who think that wherever genius is, it must, like fire, blaze out, this argument is not addressed ; but those who consider it not as a gift, but a power acquired by long labour and study, should reflect, that NO MAN is LIKELY TO UNDERGO THE FATIGUE REQUIRED TO CARRY ANY ART *to* ANY DEGREE OF EXCELLENCE, *to which, after he has done, the world is likely to pay no attention.*" (Reynolds's Journey to Flanders and Holland, p. 340, 341.)

The fact of the desertion of *West's* gallery, has been known to every artist, student, and amateur in London, for more than two years. So extraordinary a result of the great national obstacle, church exclusion, produced shame and indignation in some minds, without their well knowing whom to be angry with ; but the discouraging and alarming effect in the breasts of those who before entertained any hope of obtaining reward and distinction by historical painting, was heavy indeed. The periodical press, with well-meaning activity, had spread it abroad; not only in the united kingdom, but in foreign countries, and our rivals and competitors on the continent rejoiced in our disgrace. Thus the arts, instead of being instruments to obtain us the homage of foreign nations, became the means of dishonouring the British character. What could the people

in France, in Holland, in Italy think? What could a student hope for, when, after a long life of meritorious labours.
and professional honours, the British King's historical
painter, the President of the Royal Academy of painting,
sculpture, and architecture in London, the head of the
arts in England, an artist superior to all contemporary,
merit on the continent, and unequalled since the time of
the CARACCI, was abandoned by his country at the
close of his 82nd year, and the magnificent series of his
works deserted and left to the precarious contingencies of
the long-established anti-historical spirit produced by the
church exclusion of pictures? This, indeed, must be the
commencement of *the reign of terror* in the British School!
With what feelings of grief and apprehension must not the
students have heard those words, addressed to them with
the kindest feelings, by Sir Thomas Lawrence, the present
President of the Royal Academy, in his discourse on the
late delivery of the prizes:—" It is now more than three
years that we have witnessed at his own residence, an exhibition of the accumulated labours of this venerable and,
great master, whose remains were honoured with a public,
funeral, and whose loss was felt AS A NATIONAL CA-
LAMITY, totally neglected and deserted. The spacious,
rooms in which they are arranged, erected in just respect
to a parent's memory, and due attention to the imagined
expectations of the public, as destitute of spectators as the
vacant halls of some corporate body; and, but for the property of known value, threatening to injure the remaining
fortunes of the filial love that raised them."
Alas! with what dismay must the students have received their prizes from the Academy, with this melancholy
truth sounding in their ears like a death bell to their
hopes! Surely when artists are walled out from efforts in

T

the highest class or style of excellence, there is a danger that prizes and premiums may have the effect of multiplying the disappointments of genius, and spreading low aims and high pretensions through the land.

The purchase of the late President's magnificent collection of pictures, by a Committee appointed by Government or by Parliament, would contribute, with other measures, for giving certain employment to history painters, to terminate the reign of terror in the British School. *Aspiring* Students, if a field for emulation and constant reward were opened by the Government, would entertain a belief and reliance, that a man of genius, who devotes his life to history painting, and who obtains the highest honours of his profession by his pencil, will not be abandoned at his death; but that his interests, connected with the advancement of the arts and of the national glory, will be duly attended to by the Government after his decease, so that his family may fairly hope for a provision in the fruits of his labours and his genius. On this broad public ground the purchase would have a salutary effect in preventing the extinction of the *public* style of history in this country.

Sir Thomas Lawrence's just and feeling eulogium on Mr. West is beautifully expressed. After advising the sudents to go to his venerable predecessor's gallery for instruction, his affectionate language does honour to his head and heart. "While the extent of knowledge that he possessed and was so liberal to convey, the useful weight of his opinion in societies of the highest rank, the gentle humanity of his nature, and THAT PARENTAL FONDNESS WITH WHICH YOUTH and ITS YOUNG ASPIRINGS were INSTRUCTED and CHERISHED BY HIM, will render his memory sacred

to his friends, and ENDEARED TO THE SCHOOLS
of this Academy, while *respect for worth* and INVALUA-
BLE SERVICE *are encouraged in them.*" Here is an
irresistible claim upon his country ; his inestimable instructions and paternal affection in forming the minds of the
students in the Royal Academy during the twenty-seven
years that he was President.   Of the innumerable instances
which we have heard of his anxious endeavours to obtain
friends and patrons for young artists of merit, and to assist
them with pecuniary means, we shall close this tract with
one only, his earnest efforts to have PROCTOR rescued
from want, and sent to Italy.   Mr. Shee alludes to this
young sculptor's melancholy fate in these lines, in his
"*Rhymes on Art.*"

> "Taste views indignant pagan rites restor'd,
> And idol monsters in her shrine ador'd ;
> With holy rage each prostrate pedant spurns,
> And in a PROCTOR'S *fate* a PHIDIAS *mourns.*" :

But the deplorable end of this young artist is so well told
by Mr. Prince Hoare in his "Epochs of Art," that we
shall insert it here in his own words.   The name is, by a
typographic error, misspelt Procter in our preceding pages.

"There is yet another instance to be recorded in the
same art : but it is almost of *too pathetic* a nature to take
place in the course of common discussion.   This instance
was PROCTOR—the *victim of exalted and disappointed
hope.*   His story is extraordinary ; and it is so little generally known, that the reader will perhaps pardon digression
on the occasion.—PROCTOR was a *student in painting* in
the *Royal Academy.*   At the time of the annual competi-
tions for prizes, he, one year, presented both a drawing
and a model from the life, for the premiums of the silver
medals, and he obtained a *medal for each.*   The *present*

*President* of the Academy, *Mr. West, struck with his merit;* took proper means of communicating to him his advice to *undertake some historical subject for the next exhibition.* Accordingly, PROCTOR sent to the Academy the model of "*Ixion on the Wheel,*" which was so highly approved of by the members of the council, that it was, by their orders, placed in the centre of the library, separate from all the other models, and secured from risk of danger. The work was greatly and universally admired, and was purchased by a friendly patron of the arts.

"In the following exhibition, Proctor, encouraged by success, sent a group of "Pirithous slain by Cerberus,' which was not less admired than the former work, and was purchased by the same liberal patron.

"In a third year, conceiving his powers to be strengthened by experience, he undertook a much larger group, of "Diomedes, King of Thrace, torn to pieces by his own Horses." This masterly work obtained a degree of admiration far surpassing that bestowed on his former models, but by no means exceeding its merits. In professional judgments it *rivalled the powers of Michael Angelo, and stood inferior to Phidias alone.*—But, alas! the admirable group found no purchaser. At the close of the exhibition it was carried back to the house of the sculptor, who, stung to the heart with disappointment, instantly with his own hands broke the model to pieces." "From this period PROCTOR appeared no more at *the President's house, where he had till now become a frequent visitor.* On enquiries being made, it was reported, that he had lately been

*. Mr. WEST, who, *in the most affecting manner* related to me these anecdotes of Proctor, assured me that his sentiments of the Diomedes were such as I have stated, and that "*no praise could be too great for it.*" (Note by Mr. Prince Hoare.)

*met very meanly dressed, and apparently labouring under the greatest dejection of spirits.* A farther research ascertained, that after the unexpected neglect of his last work, he had *abandoned himself to inactivity, having taken a lodging at sixpence per night in a garret in Clare Market, supporting himself on no other food than dry biscuits, and resorting to the neighbouring pump for his only liquor. Deeply affected by this account, the* PRESIDENT *hastened to propose the consideration of Proctor's state to the council of the Royal Academy, where it was immediately moved,* that *he should be sent to Italy by the Academy, with the usual pension,* and *that fifty pounds should be moreover allowed to him* to make the necessary preparations for his journey. *This motion being carried, he was invited to dinner by his friendly protector, West;* and, *after dinner,* the *resolutions of the Academy were communicated to him. Proctor listened to the report* with *extreme emotion.* It was settled that he should instantly prepare for his journey in company *with the President's son.* Every thing conspired to elevate hope, and to promise satisfaction. The probable day of departure was named, and the grateful Proctor took his leave.

"About a week after this arrangement had been made, a friend of Proctor's, who lodged under the same roof with him, was announced at Mr. West's house. The door of the study was opened with eagerness, and the visitor was seen advancing along the gallery with tears in his eyes, and with a countenance full of sorrow and dismay : He came to relate that *poor Proctor was no more. He had suffered from no particular attack of disease ;* but HIS EXHAUSTED and LANGUID FRAME *had not been able to support the sudden reverse* which the favour of the Academy had produced in his situation and his feelings.

*The unceasing agitation of his powerful mind had over-
whelmed his strength, and he had died that morning. Such
were the talents,* and *such the history of Proctor.*—Who,
that feels for his country, will not tremble as he touches
the connecting thread of the two instances which have
just been related? Was Canova to be sought in Italy,
and Proctor to *die unnoticed at home?"* (Prince Hoare's
Epochs of the Arts, p. 79 to 84.)

We fear to annex any observation to the above affecting
and well-told narrative, lest our remarks should weaken
its deep impression. We can only add our confirmation
of the melancholy fact, that PROCTOR, who, in one year,
had obtained a prize in painting and another in sculpture,
from the Royal Academy in London, died of starvation,
or, in the words of *the Examiner,* "was *starved to death,*"
only about a year after, at, or in obscure lodgings in Clare
Market. With the inflexible pride and acute sensibility of
genius, he unfortunately had, all along, locked up the secret
of his penury in his breast as a shame, the divulging
of which would have been to him a wound worse than
death. Although of gentle manners, he could not brook
to solicit favours. But circumstances transpired after his
decease, which furnished grounds for an opinion, that the
limited sums which he had received for his model of
"Ixion on the Wheel," and twelve months after, for that
of "*Pirithous slain by Cerberus,*" the year before he exhibited his group of "Diomedes torn to pieces by his own
Horses," were the chief, if not his only, means of support
during two years. The remuneration was liberal, and was
paid by a distinguished amateur, solely as an encouragement
to a young Hercules in the arts; but it was insufficient for
his healthy sustenance and his other necessary expenses.
Intense application, enthusiastic and feverish fluctuations

between the hope of glory and the despondence arising from public neglect, joined to his scanty supply of food, gradually wore him down, and his constitution was gone before any suspicion was entertained of his real situation. If he had hinted his distress to his kind instructor and warm-hearted friend, West, he would have been saved. But the zealous efforts of that amiable man to place him in a situation in which his genius would have become an honour to his country, were defeated by his concealment of his sufferings. The honourable vote and liberal bounty of the Royal Academy, the prospect of fame and fortune, came too late: the mortal blow was struck before. Thus perished in the capital of England, in the prime of life, and in possession of the highest powers of genius, THOMAS PROCTOR, an *English Sculptor, who, if the periodical press had introduced his name and powers to the notice and patronage of his country, as the name and genius of* CHANTREY *were since, in 1805, might have lived to have been* THE PHIDIAS *of the age.*

The distinguished amateur who purchased the models of *Ixion and Pirithous* was *Sir Abraham Hume.* That gentleman was wholly unacquainted with *Proctor's* situation, but being struck by the beauties of his performances, on seeing them at the exhibition rooms, he purchased them from a liberal wish to patronise British genius. If there had been another amateur of the same discriminating taste and noble spirit to have remunerated the artist, he would have been rescued from the pangs of despair and want under which he expired. This extraordinary artist possessed a power of eye, hand, and conception beyond description. He was a native of Yorkshire, and spent his life there in the dull drudgery of a counting-house until he had past his thirtieth year. Unable any longer to resist the strong impulses within him, he came up to London, entered the

Royal Academy as a student, and broke upon the town as a meteor that dazzles and astonishes for a brief space and sinks in darkness.

Such was WEST, whose character and titles I here borrow from his contemporaries; an affectionate husband and father, a sincere friend, a benevolent good man; the founder and father of British historical painting; the King's historical painter, the greatest historic painter of the age; the President of the Royal Academy of painting, sculpture, and architecture in London; the head of the fine arts in the British empire; an honorary member of all the academies of painting, sculpture, and architecture in Europe and America; and last, but not least of his titles, the paternal guide, the able and zealous instructor, and true friend of the British students; as he appears in his kind advice, fostering encouragement, and active friendship to Proctor, whose fate he never mentioned but with emotions of sorrow and bitterness of heart. The accumulated historical labours of his pencil during a long period, are now exhibiting in the spacious rooms built at a great expense, in filial affection, and respect for the public, by his sons. We speak here from our own knowledge: if Mr. RAPHAEL and Mr. BENJAMIN WEST were possessed of an independent fortune, it would be their first pride, as Englishmen, lovers of their country, and of the British School, to follow the NOBLE EXAMPLE set by SIR GEORGE BEAUMONT, by presenting the entire collection now in their possession to the National Gallery, for the benefit of the British students, and the advancement of the fine arts. But as those gentlemen are not so circumstanced, their next pride would be to place them in the national gallery, through the wisdom and liberality of his Majesty's Government and Parliament! They now make this offer in the most open manner without any qualification or reserve whatever. After having most humbly presented a copy of these "*Observations*," to the gracious acceptance of The King, as the paternal Protector and munificent Patron of the British School, they will do themselves the honour to present a copy to each member of the two Houses of Parliament, with a ticket of invitation to view the gallery of pictures, and to judge impartially for themselves. This judgment they respectfully solicit. In these measures of due reverence to the memory of their father, they trust faithfully, and with a deep sense of unfeigned deference, to discharge a solemn duty to their country.

It would be a vain delusion for any individual to flatter himself with a thought of being able to influence a public question, where the wise and munificent efforts of his late Majesty, of the present King, and of Parliament, in their well-selected and liberal purchases of statues and pictures from "the great masters of the renowned ages," have been hitherto ineffectual. It is our pride to agree in the great principle of this subject, with all that is high and dignified in the State, and with those collective bodies which comprehend the most eminent for learning, talents, and sound thinking in the country: but we are not so sanguine nor so visionary as to indulge an expectation beyond a candid perusal, where the influence of Royalty, the weight of the Legislature, the exhortations and the liberal patronage of the British Institution, have in vain been exerted for so long a period, to move or counteract the *great national obstacle* which has for *two hundred and eighty years*, with a few rare exceptions, excluded British genius from attaining to the highest excellence in that department, in which painting is employed as a great moral instrument of national

U

improvement and renown; We are prepared for the issue, when we know that the most illustrious and powerful authorities of Government, seconded by a succession of eloquent and enlightened advocates, have not been able to change the hereditary apathy, or anti-historical prejudice of nearly three centuries, into an adoption of the *public style*, or into a sense of *its* power to command the homage of other nations, when the pencil and chisel are directed " to *produce these intellectual* and *virtuous feelings which are perpetually alive to the welfare and glory of the country.*" But far from having been disheartened by this view of the difficulties before us, it has only served to redouble our humble endeavours. We have reduced the question to its simple pacific elements, by stripping it of all those exasperations which have too often been permitted to trouble the discussion and darken the truth. We have showed that there is no just reason for casting a blame upon any of the living, or to look for secondary causes, when the great cause and impediment has existed during so many generations before us. We have drawn many circumstances out of the false light in which they have been placed, and have set them in their proper date and connection. We have respectfully enforced a truth, which future writers cannot too often repeat, that although all subordinate efforts to encourage British genius, and to give it a praise-worthy direction are highly commendable, and deserving of a zealous support, we must still remember, that, *as the power of the state under Edward VI., Elizabeth, and their immediate successors, was employed to overthrow the* PUBLIC STYLE of *painting and sculpture* in this country, so, *no inferior power, nothing but the same power, the* HEARTY EARNEST POWER OF THE STATE *under the mild and happy reign of* GEORGE IV. *is equal to the task of rebuilding the demolished fabric:* THE STATE *alone,* we repeat it, *is in possession of power to effect the desired restoration.*

It has been remarked, that he who writes in haste finds much to amend at his after leisure. We assent to this truth, and greatly fear that we have too often incurred the common lot. But, unwilling that any of our *opinions* should be imputed to others, we hope, that whatever little force of reason may be found in our views, may be attributed to the justice of the question itself, and to the merits of the great master to whose works we have adverted. We are quite willing, and it is just, if any passages in these pages be deemed blameable, that the blame shall be cast wholly on our shoulders. We make this declaration with respect to Mr. Raphael and Mr. Benjamin West as a point of truth and honour. Beyond the communication of their intentions to offer, with respectful deference, the collection of the late President to the wisdom and liberality of his Majesty's Government, and their subsequent wish to have their offer thus publicly made known, these gentlemen have not interfered in the preceding Observations. From the day of that death, which, in the feeling words of *Sir Thomas Lawrence,* " was *felt as a* NATIONAL CALAMITY," we were of opinion, that upon the fate of *the late President's unsold collection* depended *much* of the great national question, *whether the* PUBLIC STYLE *of history painting introduced and patronised by his late Majesty, would sink altogether or flourish.* We mentioned this opinion in St. Paul's Church on the day of the funeral. We are concerned to own that we entertain this opinion unaltered still. We are convinced, if *West's* unsold pictures, with all their acknowledged merits, be abandoned *to the contingencies* of the *anti-historical* and *anti-contemporarian spirit, that the* PUBLIC STYLE *must be endangered* as *to any purpose of reputation;* and with it, we greatly fear, the domestic style may gradually fall into self-imitation, and become materially enfeebled. With these serious impressions, when we were informed by Mr. Raphael and Mr. Benjamin West of their intentions, we were impelled more by our anxious good wishes than any hope of influence, SPONTANEOUSLY to offer our GRATUITOUS exertions for the purpose of setting the question on the broad grounds of reason, truth, and the imminent choice between national honour or the unavailing regret of a lost opportunity. We have endeavoured to do so without any personal interest whatever. We have had but one object in view, that of producing a general conviction of the truth for the *benefit of the public,* the patronage of British genius, and the advancement of the fine arts. To leave no possibility of further half-thinking, or misconception of the real cause which threatens the extinction of historical painting in this country, we have anxiously gone round the case on every side, and illustrated it by recapitulation, in a variety of views, all terminating in the same indisputable conclusions: by which it is plain; FIRST, that, with the domestic style, in all its branches of poetical and dramatic composition, landscape, familiar life, and portraiture, in a highly flourishing state, with the finest materials in the world for raising historical painting to its highest excellence, and with the most liberal dispositions in the breast of his Majesty, of the Government, and Parliament—the *field* of THE PUBLIC STYLE *is walled up against the exertions of British genius* by the exclusion of painting from churches, and by its exclusion from other buildings :—SECOND, that this NATIONAL OBSTACLE has operated for two hundred and eighty years as a *prevention* of *British genius in that field*; that it is now, with respect to its injurious effects, as direct a prevention and extinguisher of the *public style*, as it was in the reign of Edward VI. and Elizabeth; and that, as the power of the STATE was employed to overthrow and root out that source of patronage in this country, no inferior power, nothing but the power of the Government, can restore or rebuild it. If we would rival *Greece*, we must act upon the same high national principle on which Greece acted. Her whole system of painting and sculpture was in every sense *Greek:* it emanated from her own mighty heart and lofty spirit: it was all national, all Grecian in body and soul. Nothing that she saw in other countries had power to abate her pride in her own: she felt a national glory in the excellence of her native artists: they enjoyed a splendid public patronage, and she exulted in giving them a high place in public estimation: to be the work of a Greek artist, was, in her eyes, a merit: to be a work of excellence by a Greek artist, was a still higher claim upon her rewards and honours: but to be the HEAD OF THE ARTS IN GREECE, THE GREATEST GREEK HISTORICAL PAINTER OF THE AGE, was one of the surest claims to wealth and honour among that great and glorious people. WEST WAS SEVENTY-TWO years old when the heavy national calamity that sent him forth upon the world, without a provision, fell upon him and the empire! We ask, for his memory and his works, *as the* ACKNOWLEDGED HEAD OF THE ARTS *in the British empire*, no more than an extension of that great national principle

by which the Greek artists were enabled to set an example
of superior excellence to all succeeding ages.

The reputation of the deceased *Head of the Arts* in the
British empire belongs to his country as a portion of her
glory, and it is intimately connected with the interests of the
British School: by extending a due portion of the public
patronage to his works, on the ground of their acknowledged merits, we sustain the national honour and encourage the *living* artist. For a glorious proof of *living*
genius we refer to the rich harvest of brilliant specimens in
every class of the domestic style, *now* in the exhibition of
the British Institution. This year's display is equally honourable to the Royal Academy and British Institution,
and is a full reply to all the unthinking censures which have
been, during many years, cast upon these two bodies for
not having worked an *impossibility*. We are unwillingly
obliged to defer to another publication the critical notice
of names and pictures in the *domestic style*, which we
are proud to say, leave out of sight all contemporary
competition on the continent. In addition to these, the
few fine historical pictures by WESTALL, EASTLAKE,
NORTHCOTE, FOGGO, BRIGGS, and MARTIN, show, that
if the persevering patriotism of the British Institution had
been able to have overcome or counteracted the great national obstacle, and to have opened public edifices for the
reception of historical pictures upon a grand scale, there
would soon be joyful and able competitors for the support and glory of the *public style*. Here is a mine of
invaluable materials for the NATIONAL GALLERY, as
soon as ever a fair field shall be opened for constant employment.

We are fully aware that whoever enters into the

field of the fine arts in this country, must be prepared for defence. With this experience, we turn our eyes towards the grave of the lamented Dead, and would fain place our slender shield upon his tomb, feeling ourselves, although ill equal to the task, called upon by our sense of manliness, by our reverence for departed worth and distinguished genius, by all the public and private interests which are vested in the fame of the late President, to interpose our weak voice between his memory and any misinterpretation, let it come from what quarter it may.

THE END.

## ERRATA.

Page 35, line 6, *for* lamented *of* the, *read* lamented the.
— 45, — 26, *for* Reynolds' own, *read* Reynolds's own.
— 70, — 2, *for* cents, *read* cents."
— 86, — 8, *for* painting, *read* painting."
— 97, — 19, *for* one great, *read* our great.
— 107, — 30, *for* had far spread, *read* had spread.
— 108, — 10, *for* in the, *read* in her.

HOWLETT AND BRIMMER, PRINTERS,
10, FRITH-STREET, SOHO.

CPSIA information can be obtained
at www.ICGtesting.com
Printed in the USA
BVHW041013200819
556236BV00011B/827/P